DISCARD

VGM Professional Careers Series

CAREERS

IN MARKETING

LILA B. STAIR

VGM Career Horizons
a division of *NTC Publishing Group*
Lincolnwood, Illinois USA

Library of Congress Catalog-in Publication Data
Stair, Lila B.
Careers in marketing / Lila B. Stair.
p.   cm. — (VGM professional careers series)
Includes bibliographical references.
ISBN 0-8442-4464-3 (hard). — ISBN 0-8442-4465-1 (soft).
1. Marketing—Vocational guidance.   I. Title.   II. Series.
HF5415.122.S72   1995
658.8'023—dc20   95-779
                                                                          CIP

Published by VGM Career Horizons, a division of NTC Publishing Group
4255 West Touhy Avenue
Lincolnwood (Chicago), Illinois 60646-1975, U.S.A.
© 1995 by NTC Publishing Group. All rights reserved.
No part of this book may be reproduced, stored in a retrieval system,
or transmitted in any form or by any means,
electronic, mechanical, photocopying, recording or otherwise,
without the prior permission of NTC Publishing Group.
Manufactured in the United States of America.

5 6 7 8 9 0 VP 9 8 7 6 5 4 3 2 1

To My Daughter Leslie

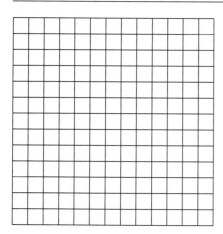

CONTENTS

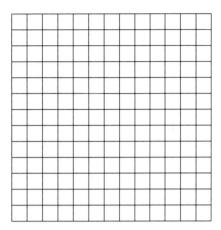

ABOUT THE AUTHOR

Lila B. Stair has an extensive background in career counseling and research. Her years as a career counselor involved both career decision-making activities as well as job development and placement. She has served as a counselor for Program for the Achievement of Competency Education (PACE), a consultant for a Washington state agency to computerize occupational services, and as a career counselor. She has also taught management and organizational behavior at Florida State University.

Ms. Stair is the author of *Careers in Business,* and *Careers in Computers,* two other titles in the VGM Professional Careers Series. She has an M.A. in counselor education from the University of New Orleans and an M.B.A from Florida State University.

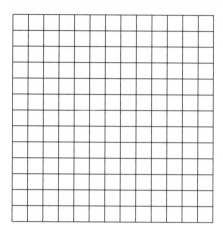

PREFACE

Choosing a career in the 1990s is somewhat bewildering because of the number and dynamic nature of the choices. An investigation of careers in marketing reveals a variety of challenging professions, including high-interest fields such as advertising as well as less well-known fields such as marketing research. Marketing attracts large numbers of people with a wide range of interests, experiences, and educational backgrounds. Of all areas open to college business and communications majors, marketing offers the widest range of career choices. The career path to the top management position in a corporation, for example, is often through marketing management. Marketing managers at all levels hold line positions with considerable power because marketing products is how companies generate revenues.

Employment with large advertising, sales promotion, public relations, and consulting agencies offers the possibility of advancement to partner, enabling an individual to share proportionately in the profits of the agency. On the other hand, marketing fields offer numerous options for self-employment as manufacturers' agents, entrepreneurs, and consultants in such areas as marketing strategy, public relations, and advertising. Whatever an individual's interests and values, marketing has something to offer.

Career decision making is one of the most difficult areas for most individuals because it requires a careful analysis of one's strengths and weaknesses and it has a major impact on one's quality of life and the achievement of personal goals. On the next page is a career decision-making model that incorporates both internal and external factors affecting career choice. The blank lines in the model enable career decision makers to add factors important to them and to rank the factors in terms of their relative importance. It was developed to enable individuals to better evaluate the career options discussed in this book.

Career Decision Making Model

Internal factors	External factors
Aptitudes and attributes	Family influence
_____ Academic aptitudes and achievement	_____ Family values and expectations
_____ Occupational aptitudes and skills	_____ Socioeconomic level
_____ Social skills	_____ _____
_____ Communication skills	_____ _____
_____ Leadership abilities	_____ _____
_____ _____	_____ _____
_____ _____	_____ _____
_____ _____	_____ _____
Interests	Economic influence
_____ Amount of supervision	_____ Overall economic conditions
_____ Amount of pressure	_____ Employment trends
_____ Amount of variety	_____ Job market information
_____ Amount of work with data	_____ _____
_____ Amount of work with people	_____ _____
_____ _____	_____ _____
_____ _____	_____ _____
_____ _____	_____ _____
_____ _____	_____ _____
Values	Societal influence
_____ Salary	_____ Perceived effect of race, sex, or
_____ Status/prestige	ethnic background on success
_____ Advancement opportunity	_____ Perceived effect of physical or
_____ Growth on the job	psychological handicaps on success
_____ _____	_____ _____
_____ _____	_____ _____
_____ _____	_____ _____
_____ _____	_____ _____
_____ _____	_____ _____

Among the factors influencing a student's career choice are expectations of family members, guidance from high school teachers, suggestions from friends, a desire to make a lot of money, and the need for prestige. A college education requires a large commitment of time, money, and energy, and selecting a college major needs careful consideration. Even students who have chosen a college major should explore other options early in their education to be sure that they have chosen wisely and avoid costly changes. Some students become dissatisfied with their original choice when they begin to take courses in the field and want to change majors. Advisors assigned to students can provide some help, but most advisors are not career specialists.

Today, most college campuses have career information centers available to both students and members of the community who are interested in exploring career options. User-friendly computerized career information systems are available in many college career centers. These systems aid students in making a career choice by relating responses on a questionnaire to various careers and generating a list of career options based on these responses. Students can then obtain descriptions of careers that look interesting. Many computerized systems provide information on colleges and financial aid as well. Career centers house numerous volumes of printed career information, including occupational briefs, current articles, and books such as *Careers in Marketing*.

It is my hope that every reader who explores marketing careers through this book will gain the insights and experience the enthusiasm for marketing that I have gained in writing it. In addition to job descriptions, this book includes personal and educational requirements for those entering marketing careers, salary data, job market information, current and future trends, job search tips, and many sources of additional information. Challenges and rewards abound for those entering the field of marketing. The first and greatest challenge is to prepare and market oneself. It is the objective of this book to help in this end.

Lila B. Stair

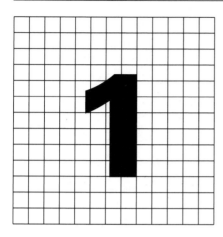

MARKETING IN TODAY'S ECONOMY

No field in business offers a greater variety of career choices than does marketing. Challenges in the field abound as marketers grapple with an economy in flux, changing tastes and values, emerging and disappearing brands, and numerous other factors that affect marketing decisions. Consumers are bombarded with information about product offerings from thousands of companies of all sizes. These companies offer far more than products. Many career opportunities are available to those prepared to take advantage of them.

Marketing is not a new field. In fact, it has been around since primitive tribes began to barter or exchange goods that were plentiful for those that were scarce. They traded grain, meat, jewelry, hides, and other items. The notion of trade existed in prehistoric times and was not so different than it is today. The board of directors of the American Marketing Association defines marketing as "the process of planning and executing the conception, pricing, promotion and distribution of ideas, goods and services to create exchanges that satisfy individual and organizational objectives." The notion of a product has been expanded to include ideas and services as well as tangible goods. As the definition suggests, marketing professionals are involved from the conception of a product that might sell to the actual sale and distribution of that product to the ultimate consumer.

The field of marketing has evolved over the centuries. The early American settlers were farmers, producing what they needed to survive. By trading with other settlers and Native Americans, they were part of the production era of marketing which lasted roughly 300 years. During these years, production evolved into a custom process that provided consumers with goods of value for which they would exchange other goods, gold, or money. Initially, products were produced on customer demand. By the 1800s producers were beginning to anticipate demand and have products ready. The Industrial Revolution was in full swing by the second half of the nineteenth century, and the mass production of products began. Unlike the early part of the century when small quantities were produced and customers were geographically close to producers, mass production created the need for sales and distribution strategies.

Thus, marketing entered its *sales era* at the beginning of the twentieth century. Producers had more to sell than they had customers, so they turned their attention to sales techniques. The hard sell was born and used to the extent that consumerism allowed. Most people think of consumerism as a fairly recent phenomenon, but it actually began in the early 1900s. Legislation regulating both product quality and misleading advertising was enacted prior to World War II. However, with consumer products scarce during the war, people were happy to get what they could. But by the 1950s the economy was booming, and products were again plentiful. It was at this time that the *marketing era* began.

The marketing era is characterized by a shift from the previous sales orientation to a market orientation. Today, the primary emphasis is no longer on selling already planned and produced goods, but rather identifying customer wants and planning products to satisfy these wants. The *marketing concept* is basically a philosophy that focuses on customer wants and identified markets. Companies have found that they can create the desire for certain types of products in well-defined groups of potential customers. Thus marketing has grown into a complex and sophisticated field needing a large number of highly trained professionals to perform its many specialized functions.

THE SCOPE OF THE MARKETING FIELD

The dramatic evolution of the marketing era increased marketing's functions from advertising and selling, which dominated the sales era, to include marketing research, product development, packaging, promotion, and public relations. Marketing begins with the identification of the need for a product, which can be a good or a service, by a particular market. Marketing research specialists perform this job. Marketing researchers locate potential consumer groups, describe them in detail, find out what these consumers want, consider these wants in terms of specific products, determine if such products exist and which competing companies are supplying them, forecast what products consumers are likely to buy in the future and which competitors are likely to produce them. And that's only part of it!

Once a product is conceived to meet a potential customer's need, the idea is turned over to a product development team. Professionals under the direction of a product manager then plan the product in detail. This planning doesn't end with the product itself but includes its price, packaging, and distribution. Product management is involved in all other marketing functions.

Additional information may be required from marketing research throughout the planning phase. Ideas for promoting the product may come directly from the product specialists.

There are three major ways to promote a product: advertising, personal selling, and sales promotion. Advertising is a nonpersonal presentation using a variety of media such as television, radio, newspapers, magazines, handbills, and billboards. Personal selling involves direct customer contact. Sales promotion, a concept born of the marketing era, involves three levels of product promotion: consumer promotion, trade promotion, and sales force promotion.

Public relations (PR) is a marketing function completely separate from advertising and sales promotion. The work of public relations personnel is to project a positive company image and to create good will with the public. Within this public are groups of potential customers. Consumerism is alive and well in today's economy. Consumer watchdogs regularly publicize business practices with which they don't agree. For instance, the tuna company that kills dolphins earns the ill will of environmentalists and others who love dolphins. One of the most effective uses of public relations today is demonstrated by environmentalists who have taken on the responsibility of monitoring the effects of both products and production processes on the environment and publicizing the results. Manufacturers must, in turn, mount public relations campaigns to counter charges and maintain a positive image.

Not for profit organizations use many of the same marketing tactics as profit-seeking businesses. The marketing concept has been effectively employed by various nonbusiness groups such as charities, the arts, educational institutions, federal and local governments. When a nonprofit organization is soliciting funds or promoting ideas, it functions in much the same way as a business selling goods or services. The expanded scope of marketing in society today accounts for the many jobs available to those with marketing backgrounds.

AN OVERVIEW OF MARKETING CAREERS

An understanding of the variety and quantity of different careers in marketing can be gleaned from the breadth of the marketing function itself. Figure 1.1 shows key management positions and functional areas in the field of marketing and how they relate to one another. Corporate management positions are discussed in chapter 8.

Marketing Research   Approaching the functional areas chronologically in terms of the marketing process, the first major area is marketing research. Manufacturers must learn whether consumers will buy a proposed product before committing huge amounts of time and money to develop and introduce it. This is the work of

Figure 1.1 Management of Marketing Functions

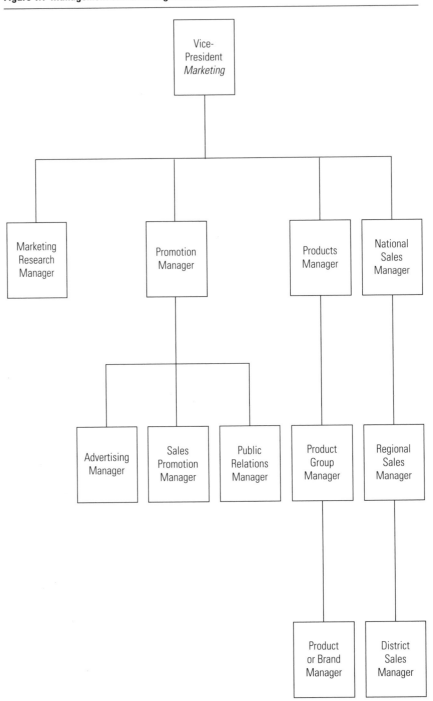

marketing research professionals. The marketing research department of a company includes the director of marketing research, researchers, and trainees. These individuals generally have degrees in marketing with strong backgrounds in statistics and psychology. Marketing researchers may also work in marketing research firms or as independent consultants. The field of marketing research will be explored in chapter 2 along with the specific duties of these professionals.

Product Development

Once an industrial firm makes a commitment to developing a specific product, a product manager is assigned or hired to spearhead the project. This position is often entitled brand manager in firms producing consumer products. The manager assembles a development team whose members work first with marketing researchers to further define the characteristics of the product, then with engineers in the design and production phases of product development, with advertising and sales promotion professionals, and finally with the sales personnel. Members of the product development team are involved in naming, packaging, and distributing the product. They usually come from different departments throughout the organization. As team members, they are in a unique position to interact with almost every department in the company. Product development can be an excellent avenue of advancement to other positions within the company because it is very visible. Chapter 3 details the work of the development team from the inception to the completion of the project.

Advertising

Of all marketing careers, advertising is perhaps the most competitive. Whether employed by a company or an advertising agency, professionals must work in a highly charged atmosphere with extreme pressure to produce. In a company, the advertising manager determines how to spend the advertising budget. Creative personnel design and produce the advertisements. These ads are then turned over to media professionals who plan marketing strategy, buying air time on television or radio and space in the print media. Research professionals study consumers' perceptions of products and advertising effectiveness, interacting with creative and media personnel in the initial production of ads and in subsequent modifications of ad campaigns. The advertising manager must decide for each product whether to conduct the ad campaign completely in-house or to hire an outside advertising agency. Advertising professionals employed by agencies perform the same functions as described above. Normally advertising agencies have four departments: creative, media, research, and account services. In the account services department an account executive oversees the entire ad campaign and serves as the liaison between the agency and the client. Chapter 4 describes an especially wide range of advertising positions with varying backgrounds and duties.

Sales Promotion

In addition to advertising, sales promotion and public relations campaigns generate sales. These two areas are completely separate and have totally different objectives. Closely linked to advertising, which is a nonpersonal presentation, sales promotion targets individual consumers. Advertising suggests and sales promotion motivates. Sales promotion falls into three categories: (1)consumer promotion, including samples, coupons, rebates, games, contests, and other incentives; (2)trade promotion for intermediaries, including cooperative ads, free goods, and dealer sales contests; and (3)sales force promotion, including such incentives as sales meetings, contests for prizes, and bonuses. Specialists in sales promotion have previous sales or advertising experience. These professionals may be employed by producer companies or sales promotion houses, which play a role similar to advertising agencies as discussed in chapter 4.

Public Relations

Both sales promotion and advertising focus on specific products. The sale of all products in a company may be improved through the creation of goodwill. The mission of the public relations department is to build and maintain a positive image of the company. Large companies have public relations departments with staffs of specialists who work under a director of public relations. Smaller companies may employ one individual to conduct public relations activities. Some companies hire public relations firms that function in the same manner as advertising agencies or sales promotion houses. Public relations personnel provide information about the organization to news media, arrange speaking engagements for company officials, and usually write the speeches. Individuals need not have marketing degrees to enter public relations; in fact, public relations people tend to come from an incredibly wide variety of backgrounds. However, they are all involved in selling—selling the company to the public. That public relations easily fits into the marketing effort of a company can be seen in chapter 5.

Distribution and Sales

The combined efforts of advertising, sales promotion, and public relations professionals create consumer awareness of a company and its products. The producer must then choose how to move its products from warehouses to these consumers. This process, called distribution, may be done through various channels. Options include the sale of the product to wholesalers, retailers, or directly to the consumer.

Sales and customer service are the keys to running a successful business in today's economy. Professional sales people are the backbone of any company. Without an effective sales force, a company could not survive in a competitive environment. With so many similar products, it is the sales force that makes the difference. Many marketing graduates start in sales. Sales is a perfect area for beginners to learn their company's business and make contributions to profits. It is an opportunity where hard work really does pay off both in increased earnings and in recognition.

Retail sales involves selling to the end user in stores of all sizes. Wholesale and industrial sales personnel sell both finished products and basic materials to retailers, other intermediate agents, and manufacturers. Industrial sales representatives are employed by manufacturers; however, they are not the only ones selling the company's products. Manufacturers' representatives are independent business people who may sell one or more companies' products to many different customers. Finally, self-employed wholesale dealers find needed products for client companies. Chapters 6 and 7 cover wholesaling and retailing.

Direct marketing or nonstore selling is growing at a faster rate than in-store selling and includes such methods as direct selling, direct response retailing, database marketing, direct mail, and telemarketing. Direct marketing offers a variety of career opportunities and will be discussed in chapter 6.

Marketing careers are varied and interesting. Depending on a person's verbal or quantitative strengths, interests, creativity, sales flair, and initiative, one of these careers could be a wise choice and provide opportunities for success. After gaining more in-depth information on all of these careers, individuals will be better able to choose a specific area within the field of marketing that is compatible with both their interests and aptitudes.

TRENDS AFFECTING MARKETING CAREERS

Marketing occurs in an ever-changing environment to which marketing professionals must adapt. The economy of the 1990s will be bolstered by a number of knowledge-driven industries including computer hardware, computer software, film and TV production, financial services, medical research, telecommunications, and tourism. The leading job creators in 1993 were the entertainment and recreation industries adding 200,000 workers, 12 percent of all net new employment, surpassing the health care industry that was the top job creator throughout the 1980s.

According to some estimates, the economy has a long-term growth potential of between 2.0 and 2.5 percent a year. To maintain a noninflationary growth rate, the Federal Reserve Board has raised short-term interest rates and is keeping a wary eye on prices. Positive economic signs include a surge in productivity, an increase in the number of highly skilled workers, efficient capital investment, expanding international trade, more affordable and useable information technologies, and an increase in patent applications. Productivity in both the manufacturing and service sectors is on the rise. Many new graduates entering the job market must be prepared to enter the service sector. According to *Fortune* magazine, growth in the largest U.S. service corporations exceeded that of their industrial counterparts by $31.1 billion in 1993.

Marketers in the 1990s will operate in a highly price-conscious environment where customers have greater and more convenient access to information. In this environment, customers should be viewed as assets and customer service as the means of retaining those assets. The marketing of both goods and services will focus on value to the customer and customer service, concepts that will be discussed in detail in chapter 5.

The markets of the 1970s changed dramatically with the introduction of new technologies, the flood of imports, and the deregulation of the airlines and other industries. The turbulent 1980s was a decade of mergers and acquisitions as organizations attempted to remain profitable or grow through restructuring.This upheaval created opportunities for entrepreneurs who found market niches, or small groups of consumers, with unfilled needs for specific goods or services. Record numbers of small businesses were created to meet these needs. Hence, the 1980s was also a decade of entrepreneurial boom. Chapter 10 describes opportunities for entrepreneurs, educators, and consultants.

During the 1990s the economy has again experienced major changes. The passage of the North American Free Trade Agreement (NAFTA) and the recently revised General Agreement on Tariffs and Trade (GATT) removed many trade barriers both in Europe and Asia and fueled the economic globalization already well underway. Improvements in network information technology and their impact on our knowledge-based economy have caused businesses to struggle to stay current in both strategy and practice. New ways of organizing work to take advantage of the improved technologies changed the nature of many jobs. Corporate leadership in such major corporations as IBM, Eastman Kodak Company, and Apple Computer, Inc. changed hands in 1993.

Changing lifestyles and values have made a dramatic impact on markets and products. The increasing number of working women has contributed to the success of stores that offer the convenience of quick shopping with no check-out lines. However, some economists assert that labor-force participation rates for women under 25 have been declining for several years and participation rates for women 25 to 44 have leveled off. More time to shop and less money to spend could hurt sales of brand name products and high-priced apparel for working women.

A more health-conscious public is demanding food with lower fat content. New fat-free products appear daily on grocery shelves. Though fast food restaurants have introduced some fat-reduced and grilled items, we still don't see veggi-burgers on many menus. One dilemma that market researchers and product developers have is distinguishing what people say they want and what they will actually buy. The success of the new Outback restaurant chain that features steak and batter fried onions in huge portions is evidence of this.

Marketers who focused attention on the young for decades have realized that the number of Americans between the ages of 25 and 34 will decrease by over one million by the year 2000 and that those 45 to 64 years of age will make up roughly 22 percent of the total population. Another 12.8

percent will be over the age of 65. Average life expectancy is currently 81 years for men and 85 years for women and is predicted to increase in future years. Many aging Americans are both physically and financially healthy. They want a variety of products and services tailored to meet their needs. The senior citizen market will receive much attention from marketing professionals in future years.

A fast-growing area of marketing is *cause marketing*. In 1993 companies spent nearly $1 billion on cause marketing campaigns, calling attention to causes and their products. Ben & Jerry's, the ice cream maker, gives away 7 1/2 percent of its pretax profits in support of environmental preservation. Coors Brewing has pledged $40 million over the next five years to fund literacy organizations. Kraft General Foods donates 25 cents to African-American student scholarship programs when consumers use specially marked coupons to purchase products. American Express raised $5 million for the antihunger organization Share Our Strength by donating 2 cents from every transaction during one holiday season. Though critics accuse some companies of using cause marketing strictly for public relations purposes, a survey reported that 66 percent of those surveyed, 1,981 consumers, said that they would be likely to switch brands if the cause was of concern to them.

Opportunities in international marketing will increase as firms respond to the invasion of imports with aggressive selling into foreign markets. As American business moves abroad, the need in all areas of marketing for individuals who are familiar with foreign languages and cultures will grow substantially. Global marketing will be the key term in the 1990s and those who are prepared to assume a role in it will find excellent career possibilities. Opportunities in international marketing will be discussed in chapter 9.

The following chapters address the impact of trends on specific areas of marketing. Successful career preparation requires mastering knowledge and skills in a discipline and educating oneself to compete in the current job market. The job market today is a function of the total marketing environment, which encompasses the trends above and many more.

THE DEMAND FOR MARKETERS

Marketing is a huge field, and marketing professionals should number more than twelve million by the year 2000 according to the Bureau of Labor Statistics. Marketing professionals are employed throughout the country by manufacturers, retailers, advertising agencies, consulting and public relations firms, product testing laboratories, and business services firms, among others. While demand for new college graduates varies from position to position and industry to industry, recent studies show that the demand for graduates in marketing or sales is the third greatest of all areas. Still, competition for many entry level positions can be quite keen.

The aging of America is having an impact on the job market. Though many baby boomers are financially well-off enough to retire early, they are also healthy enough to work longer. It is, therefore, unclear what the overall picture will be in the future regarding older people in the workforce. The media have featured many stories about the conflicting values of Generation X-ers born between 1965 and 1978 and baby boomers born between 1948 and 1964. The film *Reality Bites* addresses the current job market problems of Generation X-ers. Not only does the film depict the difficulty of finding a good job, but it shows the value conflicts between older and younger employees. Network television news also focused on this problem through a series of workplace interviews. Until baby boomers vacate the decreasing number of management positions, advancement opportunities will be limited for many entering the workforce today.

Given our ongoing transition to an information society, the nature of jobs is unclear. The new technology tools will make some jobs more interesting and demanding and others less so. Many workers will find their work means attending to machines. Karl Albrecht, author and consultant, speculates that only about 15 percent of workers are "thinkers" while the rest are "doers." Tomorrow's information age workers must objectively look at work to determine into which category specific jobs fit and whether a job affords challenge and opportunities for advancement.

In order to compete in the marketplace, many employers have attempted to reduce payroll costs by hiring temporary employees. These employees usually earn less money and have no company benefits. In the past temporary help was mostly clerical. Today, however, temporary employment agencies can provide a production line for a month or a computer team for a lengthy project. This employer option makes the job market even tighter for the first time job seeker. On the other hand, temporary employment is a way for beginners to gain some experience.

The demand and variety in marketing careers suggest that marketing has much to offer. Marketing itself is so diverse that most individuals with the resources to attend college can find jobs well-suited to both their skills and their interests. A recent article in *Sales & Marketing Management* reported the results of interviews with marketing majors at California State Polytechnic University and at the University of Southern California. Many said they chose marketing because it offered creativity, challenge with change, and variety. They expect marketing to place a greater emphasis on both identifying consumer needs and wants and on services. An investigation of careers in marketing will point out not only specific areas of opportunity, such as those outlined above, but the broader nature of marketing. Our exploration of marketing careers begins at the start of the marketing process: marketing research.

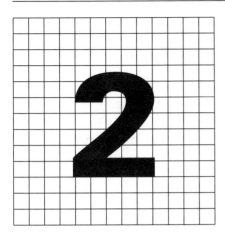

CAREERS IN MARKETING RESEARCH

What's hot—IBM PCs, Detroit, Internet, Sears, Letterman, RuPaul, Ice beer, rotisserie chicken, donuts, Shaq, health reform! What's not—PC clones, Tokyo, Madonna, dry beer, croissants, Chinese takeout, Leno, Ninja Turtles! Identifying current fads and future trends, what consumers are buying now and what they will buy in the future—this is the challenge facing marketing researchers. They use surveys to gather reams of information. For example, 67 percent of Americans responding to *Prevention* magazine's annual auto-safety survey state that safety is the most important factor when buying a new car, but large numbers of buyers don't understand how air bags work or know that traffic fatalities have declined for the fifth year in a row.

Buying habits reveal that fear of harm is a primary motivator for consumers. In recent years we have witnessed purchases of home and car security alarm systems, handguns, and nonlethal crime deterrents such as defensive sprays. Marketing researchers must constantly monitor consumer knowledge, attitudes, values, needs, demographics, and all other social components that affect what goods and services people buy. Marketing research is the primary means for determining which products the sponsoring company will offer for sale.

In order to grow, companies must use their resources to increase the sales of existing products and introduce new ones. One of the most important decisions facing marketing managers is whether or not to develop a new product. Successful new products have the potential to generate huge profits for a company. On the flipside, products that fail in the marketplace can be a company's undoing. Because the cost of developing and launching a new product in today's competitive market is enormous, most companies cannot afford too many failures. And failures do occur. Sometimes products that we like suddenly disappear from the shelves. Good products that are ineffectively marketed can be as unprofitable as inferior products that should never have been produced. Success depends on the entire marketing process working as it should, and it all begins with marketing research.

THE MARKETING RESEARCH PROCESS

Accurate and timely information is vital to the marketing research process. Many firms have taken a systems approach to marketing information. Advances in computer technology enable orderly collection, analysis, and dissemination of the information that managers need to make decisions. Managers specify the kind, amount, and quality of information that they require and turn these specifications over to their marketing research departments. Marketing research is basically the process of identifying and defining an opportunity, such as a target market or an unfilled need, collecting and analyzing the data relevant to this opportunity, and presenting the information to marketing managers. Although some ideas for products originate in marketing research, an idea can come from any source, including a company's competitors.

In the past, the Japanese proved the adage that "imitation is the purest form of flattery" by improving on existing products and capturing the largest share of the market. Today, however, the Japanese have moved to the forefront of high technology through sophisticated intelligence work. Japanese marketing researchers collect information on every aspect of American culture and technology, especially in research labs of American universities where ideas are germinated. At Stanford University, Japan has already funded six permanent research chairs and one visiting professorship, at an average cost of $1.2 million each. American marketing researchers will have to work hard to match this level of information gathering.

The marketing research department must not only have a clear idea of the current state of the company's customers, potential customers, and competitors, but must also look forward. Analysts must carefully monitor changing tastes and lifestyles in order to predict what people will want in the future. The growing teen market is influencing both the kinds of products coming to market and the manner in which they are marketed. Since 1992 the U.S. population aged 13 to 19 has been increasing and, these teens are spending billions of dollars on shoes, clothing, groceries, PCs, videogames, music CDs, and health and beauty aids. In 1993 America's 28 million teens spent $57 billion of their own money. That is powerful marketing clout. Called the most global market of all, teens around the world have surprisingly similar tastes and attitudes. Today's teens are characterized by adult sensibility, bizarre fashion combinations, and a passion for the newest technologies. But how long will they support such fads as Doc Marten boots, baby-doll dresses, and Stussy shirts? It is up to marketing researchers to predict next year's buying trends.

Ideas for new products come from trends identified through marketing research. Depending on the product, development can take a very long time.

For example, years of development and testing are required from the time an automobile design leaves the drawing board and the finished product hits the showroom floor. Many products are rendered obsolete during the development cycle by competitors' products or technological innovation.

THE WORK OF MARKETING RESEARCHERS

Marketing research professionals engage in a long list of research activities such as:

- Monitoring competitors
- Identifying market trends
- Developing customer profiles
- Measuring market share
- Evaluating brand images
- Designing products and packages
- Planning distribution channels
- Assisting in advertising and promotion campaigns
- Analyzing audience characteristics
- Evaluating the impact of advertising and promotion

These research activities involve collecting data from a variety of sources. Primary data are collected through original research for a specific purpose, and the process is usually very costly. Primary data can come from company personnel, actual and potential customers, or even competitors (usually without their cooperation). These data are normally obtained through observation, experimentation, or survey. One favorite method is to observe and record consumer behavior in stores. Experimentation may also include taste tests. Measuring the effect of advertising, price changes, and product or packaging alterations on consumer buying practices is another type of experimentation. Researchers conduct surveys by mail, telephone, or in person to get consumer reactions to existing or proposed products. Secondary data have been previously collected by individuals inside or outside the firm and may be part of company records or a large government database. Since secondary data are usually less expensive and faster to acquire than primary data, researchers normally begin the research process by collecting and analyzing all relevant secondary data.

Marketing research provides management with the information needed to develop a marketing strategy, including potential market share, sales, price, promotion, and channels of distribution. When companies decide to develop new products, designers develop prototypes on the basis of the marketing research; the prototypes are then tested for marketability. Marketing research professionals oversee market testing, report results, and make recommendations. Options include to abandon development, alter the product in some way, or plan the promotion strategy. One or more marketing researchers are part of product development teams and contribute vital information to the entire product development process. Product development will be discussed in detail in chapter 3.

The scope of marketing research is not limited to consumer products. Research may be conducted in such areas as environmental concerns, business decisions, political campaigns, association images, and a wide range of others. Regardless of the particular research question or problem, all research involves data collection and analysis. It may be quantitative in nature, involving numerical data, or qualitative, dealing with subjective information such as opinions and attitudes. Thus individuals pursuing marketing research as a career should have strong backgrounds in math and statistics as well as psychology.

An important influence on the field of marketing research today is database marketing. New generations of faster, more powerful computers enable marketers to build huge databases to analyze their customers. Mass marketing of the 1950s and 1960s presented the same message and product to all consumers. During the next decade mass marketing was refined to segment marketing that divided consumers into smaller groups with common characteristics. Today database marketing enables marketers to identify very small consumer niches, often individuals. Individual buying practices and preferences, acquired from warranty cards, sweepstakes entries, and any form an individual fills out when making a purchase, are entered into huge databases. Powerful software extracts common characteristics of users of specific products. The groups of consumers who share these characteristics, such as income, age, and brand preference, are identified. This information is then incorporated into the development of new products, advertising strategies, and every aspect of the marketing process. Databases are continually updated and database marketing programs are becoming essential to "business as usual."

CAREER PATHS IN MARKETING RESEARCH

Manufacturers of goods or services staff marketing research departments or hire outside firms to do marketing research. The keener the competition, the more important the role that marketing research plays. This role is further determined by the size of the organization and its need for research. In companies with marketing research departments, the director of marketing research usually reports to the marketing manager, who coordinates information from marketing research with technical research and product development. The director of marketing research works with the marketing manager in specifying research projects. These projects are then assigned to analysts who work with other members of the marketing research department in a team effort. The director decides when outside specialists are needed, hires them, and coordinates their activities with those of the internal personnel throughout the research process. Figure 2.1 shows the positions within the marketing research department or in marketing research firms that are described below.

Figure 2.1 Marketing Research Department

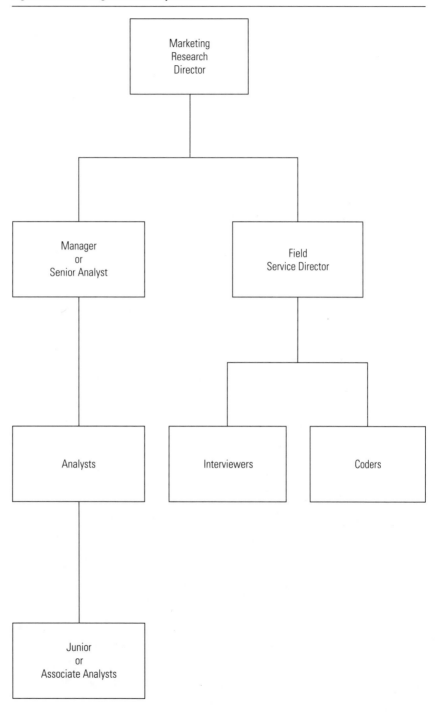

Junior Marketing Research Analyst

Typically college graduates are hired as junior or associate analysts. Although entry-level positions may involve such mundane work as handling correspondence and proofreading questionnaires, throughout the first year the junior analyst will also be involved in developing questionnaires for surveys, analyzing data, organizing studies, and writing reports. As in every job, the activities assigned to the entry-level worker depend on the worker's ability to handle the tasks and the projects currently under way in the department. Understanding that the first year is a training year, the new worker should use it as a practical learning experience and should be prepared to assume whatever duties are assigned.

Field Service Director

The field service director hires field service personnel, including interviewers and coders, to perform specialized tasks and directs their efforts. Workers in field services conduct interviews by phone or in person, asking questions that have been written by research analysts in charge of a project. Coders or tabulation personnel enter numbers into the computer and run standard programs. These programs produce the initial reports that provide the basis for further analysis. Field service and tabulations personnel usually do not need college degrees, often work for minimum wages, and do not normally advance to other positions in marketing research. College students sometimes work part time as interviewers or coders to gain experience in that aspect of marketing research.

The field service director, on the other hand, is an integral part of the marketing research process. The director may have begun as a junior analyst and been promoted. Depending on skills and performance, the field service director may be promoted to analyst or senior analyst positions. In smaller companies, interviewing and coding may be done by junior analysts. Sometimes field and tabulation work is contracted out to field service firms. The director of field services handles any arrangements, contracts, and communications with these firms.

Marketing Research Analyst

Once junior analysts demonstrate an understanding of the research process and the ability to analyze data and relate conclusions to the specifics of the project, they are promoted to the position of analyst. A marketing research analyst works with managers to gather background material and develop proposals for research projects. Analysts with two or three years of experience work fairly independently on their own projects. Communicating tactfully and courteously with managers regarding pet projects is vital to career success. Sometimes research reveals that certain projects are not viable. The analyst must present these results as thoroughly and professionally as possible. Although number crunching is an important part of marketing research, human relations skills are equally important.

Senior Marketing Research Analyst

After four or five years, successful analysts may be promoted to senior analyst or marketing research manager. Senior analysts may spearhead research projects or function as advisors for other analysts. Although one senior analyst is responsible for each project, the analyst may confer with other senior analysts as needed for suggestions or solutions to problems that arise during the project. Marketing research involves teamwork. The senior analyst supervises the work of junior analysts, coordinates the input of everyone involved in the project, and presents the conclusions. The senior analyst works with, and sometimes under, a research manager. This manager serves in a consulting capacity and, if employed by a marketing research firm, may well have been the individual instrumental in getting the client's business. An important part of the senior analyst's job in marketing research firms is obtaining new accounts and maintaining contacts with new clients.

Marketing Research Director

The director of the marketing research department in a company holds the top position and its requisite responsibilities and headaches. In the capacity of director, an individual is the liaison between the department and the rest of the company. Staffing the department, preparing the budget, overseeing all projects, and reporting to the marketing manager periodically are all part of the job. In marketing research firms, the top position—president of the firm—is usually held by the owner or a partner. In this role, bringing in new business is a vital part of the job. The head of a firm is also concerned with satisfying the demands of clients rather than upper-level management. However, whether marketing research is done in a department or by a marketing research firm, the activities performed by analysts are basically the same.

Regardless of the position held, professionals in marketing research work under a certain amount of pressure. An analyst may work on more than one project at a time and face multiple deadlines. Since analysts are assigned total responsibility for projects, the buck stops with them. They are highly accountable for success or failure even though, as in all research, some variables are beyond their control. As an analyst, one is subject to the priorities of others. For example, the marketing manager may dictate the analyst's schedule, requiring the analyst to stop work on one project at a crucial time and take on something else deemed more urgent by upper management. Nonetheless, the work is both challenging and rewarding. Marketing researchers are the pioneers of marketing—exploring new possibilities that sometimes result in revolutionary new products that make life easier or more enjoyable.

OPPORTUNITIES IN MARKETING RESEARCH

The growth in the field of marketing research is a testimonial to its effectiveness. All kinds and sizes of businesses are engaged in marketing research.

Hospitals use marketing research to project growth; colleges, to target potential students and allocate resources among academic areas; and nonprofit organizations, to determine who contributes and how best to solicit donations. Large manufacturers of consumer goods staff marketing research departments, but major growth in the field is occurring in the increasing numbers of independent research firms. Some of these firms employ as many as forty people, but most are small and often specialize, for example, in educational institutions, hospitals, nonprofit organizations, or a particular type of consumer good or service. Expanding service industries such as financial and business services, cable television, health, and leisure activities use marketing research firms. Two major retail tracking firms supply information on how well various products are selling and where: A.C. Nielsen Company, which pioneered retail tracking in the 1920s, and Information Resources, which is a relative newcomer to the field. It is wise for those interested in marketing research to develop career objectives with some area of specialization in mind.

Advances in information technology and the commitment of top management to having timely and accurate information have contributed to growth in the field of marketing research. Today, more powerful computer hardware and software analyzes data in a fraction of the time required in the past. Sophisticated multivariate statistical analyses yield information too cumbersome to derive using manual means. This type of analysis takes some of the guesswork out of producing and marketing new products. As both domestic and foreign competition place more pressure on companies to produce successful products, managers will rely more and more on marketing research information to make their decisions.

Though job openings will grow at a faster-than-average rate, competition will be tough. An undergraduate degree is required for entry into marketing research. This degree may be in any of a number of areas including statistics, psychology, computer science, marketing, or another business major. The particular major is less important than skills in math, statistics, computers, research design and analysis, and both written and oral communications. As mentioned above, a career objective that focuses on a specific industry in which the applicant has knowledge or experience is helpful. The best chance for a beginner to break into the field is to gain relevant experience as a student through jobs in interviewing or data entry, involvement in research projects, directed independent study, or (best of all) an internship in a marketing research department or firm. Internships in marketing research are not easy to find. Sometimes leads on internships can be obtained from trade associations and college placement offices.

Salaries of marketing research professionals vary considerably according to the size of the firm, level of responsibility, geographical location, and other factors that will be discussed in chapter 11. Figure 2.2 gives an average annual salary for some marketing research positions.

Figure 2.2 Annual Salary for Marketing Research Positions

Marketing Research Director	$64,000
Assistant Director	56,000
Senior Analyst	45,000
Analyst	34,000
Junior Analyst	26,000
Field Work Director	29,000

SOURCES OF INFORMATION

Trade associations are an excellent source of up-to-date career information. A partial list of marketing research organizations appears below.

>Marketing Research Association
>2187 Silas Deane Highway, Suite 5
>Rocky Hill, CT 06067
>(202)257-4008
>"Employment and Career Opportunities in Marketing Research", free publication

>The Chemical Marketing Research Association
>60 Bay Street, Suite 702
>Staten Island, NY 10301
>(718)876-8800
>"Careers in Industrial Marketing Research", free publication

>The Life Insurance Marketing Research Association
>Box 208
>Hartford, CT 06141
>(203)677-0033

CAREERS IN PRODUCT DEVELOPMENT

Every year fascinating new products enter the marketplace. *Business Week* magazine asks its editors to nominate best new products each year. In 1993 some of best products were the new Dodge Ram pickup truck, Sharp Viewcam camcorder, Compaq Presario personal computer, Media Vision Inc.'s new interactive games *Oceans Below* and *Quantum Gate*, Fitness Master FM570 stairclimber, Lego construction sets, Hewlett-Packard's 2.9-pound OmniBook PC, Black & Decker's PowerShot heavy-duty stapler, Ford's new Mustang, Cannondale's Super V mountain bike, Intel's Pentium microprocessor, Wilson Sporting Goods Company's Sledge Hammer tennis racket, Mitsubishi Electronics America Inc.'s Table Top Big Screen projection TV, and Timex Corporation's Indiglo, the watch whose face glows in the dark and helped people trapped in the World Trade Center during the bombing. These products are **truly** new and improved and represent only a small fraction of the plethora of new products introduced during that single year. *Fortune* magazine mentions some of the same products on its "products of the year" list and includes others such as Arizona Iced Tea, Barney, *The Bridges of Madison County*, and the multiple sclerosis drug Betaseron, to mention a few.

Products are conceived with markets in mind. For example, companies are continually introducing a host of new products to capture the 4- to 12-year-old market. Clothes, books, videogames, movies, television shows, greeting cards, and all sorts of new products designed to appeal to that age group will continue to flow into that steadily expanding market. Many older parents, both working, have more money and only one to two children to spend it on. A dip in the divorce rate suggests greater affluence in two-parent families. It is the job of market researchers to document and interpret these trends and suggest new products or marketing strategies to exploit them.

The constant demand for new products is the force that drives product development efforts. Companies try to give consumers what they want, when and where they want it, at a price they are willing to pay. This involves management decisions pertaining to the marketing mix or the four P's: product, place, promotion, and price. Marketing managers assemble product development teams to help make these essential decisions and shepherd a product through the development process. Whether companies can survive and profit in the competitive marketplace depends on the effectiveness of these teams.

THE PRODUCT DEVELOPMENT PROCESS

One of the most prolific companies in the area of new product development, Rubbermaid, was number one in Fortune Magazine's "Most Admired Company" survey. This manufacturer of over 5,000 products introduces new products at a rate of nearly one per day, with nine out of ten successes, and this figure does not include the products that are improved versions of older products. Who generates all of these product ideas? Twenty teams of five to seven people from a variety of departments such as marketing, manufacturing, research and development, and finance. Even top management does its share. Two top executives touring the British Museum's Egyptian antiquities exhibit returned to the U.S. with eleven ideas for new products. Along with a variety of kitchen and bath utensils, mailboxes, storage containers, cleaning aids, and tackle boxes, Rubbermaid also offers a variety of products for the youth market including toys, makeup organizers (with a free CD per purchase), litterless lunchboxes, and Sip 'n Saver drink bottles. The latter two also appeal to the environmentally conscious.

Product development sometimes involves developing an entire line of products. Black & Decker took notice of the rapid expansion of the Home Depot chain of stores and the popular sitcom, *Home Improvement*. Sales of home improvement products generated nearly $73 billion in 1992, and that sum is projected to increase 6.3 percent each year for the next five years. To capitalize on the do-it-yourself market, Black & Decker introduced its Quantum line of eighteen power tools in August of 1993 with a $10 million advertising campaign. In response to consumer interest surveys, Black & Decker offers PowerSource for free maintenance checks on all tools and a toll-free hotline where experienced advisors answer home repair questions from 7:00 A.M. to 10:00 P.M. seven days a week.

The product development process consists of a series of stages. Figure 3.1 shows the stages.

Idea Generation   The first stage of product development is conceiving ideas for potential products. These ideas come from a variety of sources. Large firms have research and development (R & D) departments whose goal is to keep the firm competitive through the identification of potential new products or the modification of existing ones. R & D is especially vital in high-tech industries

Three

Figure 3.1 The Product Development Process

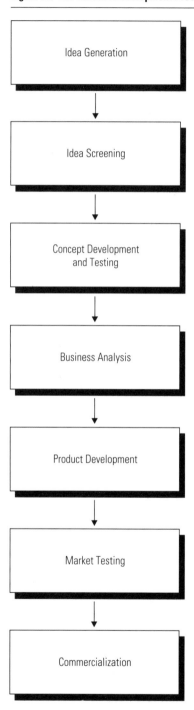

that must remain on the cutting edge of technology in order to stay in existence. Other sources of ideas within the company include executives, sales and service personnel, production workers, and marketing researchers. Ideas also come from external sources like trade journals, competitors, and customers. Sometimes inventors approach companies with ideas for products.

Products can be totally new concepts, extensions of other products, or "new and improved" versions of old products. Cable radio was born from cable television; new Cheerios are crispier to ward off sogginess; new Wheaties have a milder, whole-grain flavor; Sprint and Visa International have launched a new calling-card service that offers discounts on long distance calls made with Visa cards. A new microwave clothes dryer is now in the development stage, but such problems as what to do about metal objects left in the pockets (they would burn the clothes) must be solved. Sometimes a new use for an old product can be marketed with positive results. For years horse owners have used Straight Arrow's Mane'n Tail horse shampoo on their own hair, claiming it made their hair softer and gave it more body. Today, Straight Arrow sells two-thirds of its products for human use through outlets like Wal-Mart.

Idea Screening

Ideas must be evaluated in terms of the company's existing products, markets, and resources. Some of the questions that must be addressed follow. Will the product fit into the company's current product line ? Can it be sold to existing customers or must new markets be developed? Will additional personnel be required to develop the product? Must the sales force be re-trained? Will plant expansion be necessary? Can the product be distributed through existing channels? How quickly can development costs be recaptured? Can the product be advertised and promoted through currently used media? Is it protectable by patent? Marketing managers consider many factors during the screening stage, but the basic consideration is whether potential profits will outweigh production costs.

One pitfall of introducing new products into any existing product line is cannibalism, a situation in which the new product actually takes sales away from the existing products. When Gillette introduced Sensor, its new permanent razor, the company's market share in disposable razors declined. However, even though Sensor cannibalized other Gillette sales, its higher price resulted in higher profit margins.

Pricing in today's economy has had a major impact on new products. With inflation under control and cost-conscious consumers in the stores, there is a trend toward producing quality products, with fewer of the extra features that customers don't really value, and offering them at a lower price. Instead of pricing products in the traditional way, adding a profit margin to the cost of producing a product, companies are setting a target price for a new product. Then the product is designed with that price in mind. In the fast food industry, for instance, most companies have introduced items priced under one dollar in order to appeal to younger consumers. The resurgence of the 47-cent Krystal burger, so popular in the 1950s, is witnessed by the new stores appearing around the country.

Concept Development and Testing

Ideas that pass the screening process are turned over to marketing research professionals who describe the concept to potential customers and analyze their reactions to it. Do they like it? Would it be useful to them? What characteristics of the product do they like and dislike? Would they buy it? How would they change it to make it better? From this research a concept emerges. This product concept then undergoes business analysis.

Business Analysis

Many products never go beyond the concept stage because, despite their merits, they would not provide the firm with enough profits to justify development costs. Demand analysis, or forecasts of market and sales potential, must be measured against a cost analysis that considers R & D, production, and marketing costs. If the product still looks good after this analysis, it enters the product development stage.

Product Development

Working together, the R & D and engineering departments develop a prototype of the product. Only if the prototype tests as expected in terms of performance, quality, and safety is it slated for market testing.

Market Testing

Conventional market testing is done in one or two sample cities chosen because they represent the larger market for the product. Because of the high costs of this type of testing, companies sometimes hire outside research firms to run mini-market tests for certain retail items. These companies arrange to have stores place the product on their shelves to see how it is received by consumers. Some tests are run in laboratories where subjects are shown ads and promotion materials along with the product. Subjects are taken to mock or real stores, and researchers monitor their buying behavior. Computer analysis of the test results determines whether the product has been received as expected. If so, it enters the commercialization stage.

Despite elaborate testing, problems can arise after a product is introduced. For instance, before Unilever introduced a manganese-based detergent 60,000 consumers tested the product over a three-month period. Nevertheless, the company was forced to reformulate this powder to combat a charge from an independent consumer organization that claims its own test shows that cotton clothes are weakened over time by the new detergent. Critics say that Unilever's tests were conducted over too short a time period and with towels made of linen, a very tough fabric. Therefore, each stage in the product development process must be carefully planned if the product is to be successful.

Commercialization

This is the stage at which the marketing organization operates at full power to develop a marketing strategy for the life of the product. Activities involving production, distribution, sales, advertising, and promotion personnel are coordinated as the product enters production, Technically, this last stage of product development is the first stage in the product life cycle as seen in figure 3.2. The figure shows how a product is introduced, grows, matures, and declines. When sales of a product start to decline, the company often introduces the "new, improved" version. Sometimes repositioning can revitalize product sales. For example, Proctor & Gamble introduced Pampers Phases, disposable diapers with different design and absorbency for the four stages of the child's early years. These diapers may actually be identical to the "small," "medium," and "large" Pampers that have been sold for years. However, renaming the product to call attention to its relation to a child's growth stages may well attract new customers. Implicit in the product life cycle is the continuing need for new products or marketing strategies and for the people who develop them.

The Importance of Brands

Anyone who thinks that the appeal of brand names is declining probably doesn't have a teenager in the house. Brands have always played an important role in the product offerings of companies. Today even the youngest consumers want clothes with labels such as Gap, Guess, Stussy, Doc Marten, depending on the current fads. Brand names suggest certain styles and qualities; they distinguish products from similar ones and often lend pizzazz to

Figure 3.2 Product Life Cycle

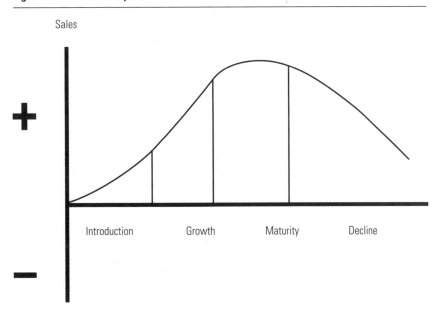

promotion campaigns. Brand identification can help or hurt products. Lacoste polo shirts with the familiar crocodile enjoyed popularity for decades. Originally the brand had considerable snob appeal, but then General Mills bought the U.S. rights to Lacoste and began using the logo on everything, including children's fashions. The French-manufactured cotton shirt changed character and appeal when General Mills began manufacturing its shirts in the Far East using cheaper synthetic blends. Lacoste began to lose market share. Exit the crocodile, and enter the polo pony as Ralph Lauren took over leadership in a market estimated at $2.8 billion. The French manufacturer Devanlay S.A. bought back the U.S. Lacoste license and is determined to restore the brand to its former status. Once again Lacoste shirts are made in France from 100 percent cotton, the brand is sold only in upscale department stores like Saks, Bloomingdale's and Neiman Marcus and shirts sell for about sixty-five dollars. Logos denoting brand names have considerable image appeal and can be a powerful advertising tool. For example, the most frequently requested tattoo in parlors across America is the Harley-Davidson logo. The key to selling a successful brand is the same as for any successful product—understanding its market!

THE WORK OF PRODUCT AND BRAND MANAGERS

The product or brand manager is assigned a product or product line that is approved for development. Determining objectives and marketing strategies for the product is part of the job description but falls short of describing the work that these managers must perform. Since product managers have no direct authority over personnel in other departments vital to their success, such as advertising or sales, they must be skilled in gaining the cooperation and support of others. It is not unusual for companies to sell products that compete with one another. In this case, a product manager must compete with other product managers within the firm for this cooperation and the necessary resources.

Product managers may be assigned to manage a product through its entire life cycle. Sometimes, however, a new-product development manager is assigned for a product's initial development and test marketing. At the conclusion of test marketing, a product manager will take over and remain in charge of the product throughout the rest of its life cycle. Working under the marketing manager, a product manager must provide the information for top-level management decisions. The responsibilities of product managers are summarized below:

1. Evaluate product testing and recommend whether to terminate development, modify product, or begin campaign.
2. Plan introduction and scheduling of the finished product and packaging with the production department.

3. Provide information and recommendations on price of product in co-operation with marketing research department.

4. Develop sales and profitability forecasts and marketing budgets with finance department.

5. Analyze statistics and recommendations from marketing research to allocate funding for advertising and promotion campaigns.

6. Identify channels of distribution, such as wholesalers, retailers, or direct sales to the public.

7. Work with marketing research and advertising agency to position product; that is, create an image of the product in the minds of consumers as having the attributes that they want.

8. Coordinate production and promotion of the product.

A less savory role in product management involves recalling products because they pose threats or hazards to consumers. When this happens a product recall manager is assigned to reverse the marketing channels that are part of the distribution process. Stock is removed from retail shelves, returned to the manufacturer, and disposed of or repaired, in the case of cars. The product recall manager oversees the entire operation.

PRODUCT MANAGEMENT TEAMS

The product manager has an assistant product manager to help in overseeing and coordinating all activities associated with the product throughout the development process and life cycle. Often the manager and assistant manager head up a product management team of specialists from all areas, including marketing research, R & D, production, advertising, sales promotion, and sales. Sometimes product managers choose their own teams; other times specialists from various areas who share an interest in a particular product volunteer to develop that product. Sometimes outside specialists are called in. Top management is committed to use whatever resources are necessary to get the job done efficiently and effectively. For this reason, there are no set formulae for personnel use. Rather, personnel assignments may vary from project to project as the situation requires.

As a product goes into development, product managers and their assistants interact with almost every department in the company. This provides excellent opportunities for learning every aspect of the company business and making contacts that could be useful in advancing to higher positions in the company.

BEYOND PRODUCT DEVELOPMENT

Three important aspects of product development that are planned and carried out with the help of specialists are packaging, distribution, and promotion.

Packaging

Packaging is an unheralded aspect of the marketing process, yet it is as carefully planned as the product itself. A package does more than hold and protect the contents of a product throughout distribution. A package also advertises and promotes the product. Clever packages can give an advantage to one product over a competing one. Growing Healthy, a new and rapidly growing manufacturer of frozen baby food, developed a two-compartment container allowing either consumption of both compartments or consumption of one compartment and convenient storage of the other for future use. The design was based on knowledge that the amount contained in jars of the competitors' food was rarely consumed in a single feeding, but rather stored in the refrigerator and often ultimately thrown away. In addition to being convenient and attractive, a package can be functional; examples include squeeze bottles for margarine, mustard, and ketchup; resealable plastic bags for cold cuts; and metal or plastic containers that can be reused.

The product development team generates ideas for packaging. Packages may be purchased from outside companies or produced in-house. Engineers design the package according to specifications from the product manager and advertising and promotion specialists.

Partly in response to environmental groups, McDonald's has begun to phase out its signature foam sandwich containers. Despite McDonald's original claim that the containers were environmentally friendly because they didn't require much space in landfills and despite the polystyrene manufacturer's industry-sponsored recycling company to which McDonald's sent its plastic refuse, quilted, biodegradable paper will replace the foam containers. According to consumers in Cleveland who tested the new paper wrap, it kept the product hot and moist. So today McDonald's is being applauded instead of being criticized by environmental groups and is helping to launch high-tech paper packaging that proponents call a breakthrough.

Distribution

Getting a product into the hands of the consumer is a vital part of the marketing effort. A small bakery sells directly to consumers, but what about a large bakery? How do bakeries get the supplies needed to produce their products? Manufacturers get the materials needed for production from suppliers. Their completed products are usually sent to intermediaries, also called resellers or middlemen. These intermediaries, either individuals or firms, may be retailers or wholesalers. They serve as a link between the manufacturer and final buyers of the product. Careers in retailing and wholesaling will be investigated in chapters 6 and 7. Producers, intermediaries, and final buyers form what is called a marketing channel or channel of distribution.

Distribution involves a host of marketing functions, including transporting and storing products and supplying market information. Since profits depend on the efficient and effective delivery of products into the hands of consumers, distribution is a carefully planned aspect of product development. As mentioned in the discussion of product screening, having channels of distribution in place is a big asset for any new product. Product or brand managers plan distribution strategy as part of the overall marketing strategy. This strategy is then implemented by a host of distribution professionals.

Promotion

The product manager works with a variety of specialists to best determine how to launch the new product on the market. There are four elements of promotion: advertising, sales promotion, public relations, and personal selling. The extent to which these elements are used depends on the industry and the product. Careers in these areas will be described in chapters 4, 5, 6, and 7.

OPPORTUNITIES IN PRODUCT MANAGEMENT

Product management is very much like running a small business. For this reason most companies assign entrepreneurial types to the job. In fact, product managers sometimes use their corporate experience to start their own businesses. Large manufacturers hire only MBAs for the entry-level position in product management—assistant product manager. Opportunities in product management in smaller companies are available to promising candidates with undergraduate degrees. The largest companies such as General Foods and Proctor & Gamble offer formal training programs. Slightly smaller companies, for example, Bristol-Myers and Johnson & Johnson, offer informal training. In small companies, training is hands-on. Slow growth in consumer goods markets will make competition for positions in product management even keener. However, opportunities are increasing in the rapidly growing field of financial services marketing.

CAREER PATHS IN PRODUCT MANAGEMENT

Promotion from assistant to product manager is the usual career track. Some companies producing dozens of brands in various categories have created a higher managerial position called category manager to which all brand or product managers in that category report. The category manager, who reports to the marketing manager, plays a vital role in determining marketing strategy for all brands in that product category. Promotions from product management, which is middle-level management, to top management are possible. Corporate marketing management will be discussed in chapter 8.

Salaries of Product Managers

New graduates hired as assistant product or brand managers earn about $25,000. Average annual salaries, not considering bonuses and benefit packages, for product and brand managers range from $40,000 to $60,000. However, this figure can be considerably higher depending on the importance of the product under development. The larger the amount of company resources budgeted for product development, the more important the role of the product manager and the higher the salary. Other factors that affect salaries will be discussed in chapter 11. The best chance of landing the most desirable positions is to find an internship or cooperative program while still in college. This experience is the key to the best jobs in all areas of marketing.

SOURCES OF INFORMATION

The best career planning sources of information in the field of product management are professional associations. Some of these are listed below.

> Product Development and Management Association
> Indiana University Graduate School of Business
> 801 W. Michigan Avenue
> Indianapolis, IN 46202-5151
> (317)274-4984
>
> Project Management Institute
> P.O. Box 43
> Drexel Hill, PA 19026-0043
> (215)622-1796
>
> American Management Association
> 135 W. 50th Street
> New York, NY 10020-1201
> (212)586-8100
>
> National Management Association
> 2210 Arbor Boulevard
> Dayton, OH 45439
> (513)294-0421

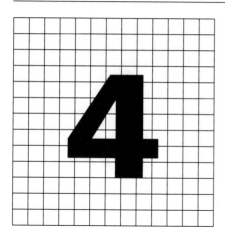

CAREERS IN ADVERTISING AND SALES PROMOTION

Promoting products through advertising and sales promotion devices is evolving as technology opens new avenues to reach consumers. Advertising is about to undergo major changes with the advent of interactive television. Once the passive recipient of information presented in TV ads, the consumer will soon use specially adapted hand-held remote devices to interact with commercial messages. For example, a shopper will be able to view a car in several different colors, ask for price, and arrange for a test drive—all via television. One prediction is that two-way TV with hundreds of channels will reach 25 percent of American households by 1997.

Advertising, technology, and marketing experts are considering new approaches, such as using infomercials that target specific consumer groups; advertising more at live events where consumers are a captive audience; revising use of both unconventional media such as in-store advertising and conventional media such as newspapers, magazines, and radio; and selling directly to consumers using the new media. Interactive TV and new media opportunities will affect many jobs in the field of advertising.

Free shares of stock with the purchase of a bag of popcorn, long-distance calling cards picturing soccer stars, an all-female baseball team—companies have been using all sorts of new techniques to promote sales. These sales promotion campaigns subtly and effectively influence the American consumer to purchase certain items. Sales promotion in combination with advertising, personal selling, and public relations comprise the product-promotion efforts. How much time and money are spent on each of these components depend on the product itself and decisions made by management. As complementary components of a campaign, advertising and sales promotion work together to win customers. Often commercials advertise promotions.

The distinction between advertising and sales promotion is that advertising suggests while promotion motivates. Signs that say, "Buy one, get one free" or a coupons that specify "Save fifty cents," motivate consumers to try the product. While advertising may go on for indefinite periods of time, sales promotion is done for a limited time period, normally when a product is first introduced. For the past couple of years, packaged-goods companies spent more dollars on consumer promotions than on media advertising. The current wave of giveaways, tie-ins, coupons, and contests is in keeping with the trend of selling to individuals rather than masses.

THE EVOLUTION OF ADVERTISING

It's interesting to consider the history of advertising and how much it has changed over the years. In the year 1878, before the existence of modern advertising and communications, three events occurred. First, a worker churned a batch of White Soap too long, making it light enough to float. Then an assay showed the soap to be 99 44/100 pure. Finally, Harley Procter sat in church musing over the words of the forty-fifth Psalm, "All thy garments smell of myrrh and aloes and cassia out of ivory palaces whereby they have made thee glad." On Monday, Procter changed the name of his soap from White Soap to Ivory Soap. The subsequent ad blitz with the familiar message, "Ivory soap. It floats," created a brand out of a commodity and a new soap empire. This and other stories may be found in *Advertising in America: The First 200 Years* by Charles Goodrum and Helen Dalrymple.

Early advertisements established the ground rules for advertising that exist to this day. However, unlike the early ads that communicated a basic selling message in an inventive but forthright manner, the ads of today use more daring techniques to avoid being lost in the barrage of media noise. As a result, many artistically exciting ads leave viewers asking themselves, "What are they selling?" The key then is to make a creative impact and sell the product. Ads that do not result in sales are failures. So creative types who opt for advertising as a career must have a business orientation.

ADVERTISING STRATEGY

The trend in advertising today is toward textbook-type advertising that stresses value and distinguishes a product from its rivals. This is true even for Apple Computer, whose dramatic, costly, high-concept ads of the early 1980s, designed to produce images linking the product to the customer, made advertising history. This is not to suggest that creative visual artists will be unable to "do their thing" in advertising. Today, the art director carries more clout than his counterpart in copywriting. However, in leaner times, companies are more likely to take a safe approach than to risk hundreds of thousands of advertising dollars on a radical new concept ad.

An effective advertising strategy is critical to the successful launch of new products. Basically, advertising involves the creation and placement of information designed to increase sales in mass media such as television, radio, newspapers, magazines, and billboards. The total advertising effort to introduce and stimulate additional sales of a product is called an advertising campaign and involves numerous advertising professionals working in a variety of capacities. Often considered the glamour job of marketing, advertising is in fact highly competitive and very hard work. However, for creative individuals who can stand the pressure, the work is both challenging and rewarding.

WHERE ADVERTISING PROFESSIONALS ARE EMPLOYED

Advertising professionals find jobs in advertising agencies, in advertising departments of large companies (in-house advertising agencies), or with mass media as advertising sales representatives. Functions performed are similar in the first two, the obvious difference being that companies promote their own products, while ad agencies promote products for client companies who pay for their services. Both aim for success. The agency that does not produce a successful ad campaign for a client loses the account. The advertising professionals involved in unsuccessful campaigns sometimes lose their jobs. Nearly all major ad campaigns are created in advertising agencies. One-third of the ad agencies are large, employing over one thousand employees. The other two-thirds are small and often specialize. The vast numbers of advertising jobs are in independent agencies. In-house agencies do offer positions that are comparable in both responsibility and salary, and creative jobs in companies are often less competitive than those in agencies.

Another position often found in companies that sell goods and services is the marketing communications specialist. Supervised by marketing managers, these specialists act as the liaison between their company and outside firms employed to support marketing efforts such as advertising, sales promotion, and public relations firms. They articulate the company's product strategies and requirements to these firms and report progress and queries on campaigns to the marketing manager. In addition, they may have responsibilities for internal communications.

CAREERS IN ADVERTISING AGENCIES

Advertising agencies usually have four departments: account services, research, creative, and media. Jobs in advertising agencies are divided equally between account support professionals (the suits), including account services, marketing research, and media planning, and creative functions professionals (the creatives). Advancement into account services comes with experience and success in one of the other departments and can lead to management.

The Account Services Department

Just as the product manager oversees every aspect of product development, the account executive plans and monitors all activities in an ad campaign. The proverbial buck stops with the account executive, although all jobs are vulnerable when major ad campaigns are involved. This increases the pressure on the executive. An unsuccessful advertising campaign can result in a product failure for the client and the loss of a major customer for the agency. Because of the vital nature of the work in account services, only experienced individuals need apply. Account executives may be promoted from other areas in the agency or hired from other advertising agencies.

The account executive works with the client, an individual or company, in planning an advertising campaign. To assess the client's advertising needs, the account executive must be familiar with all of the client's marketing efforts and how the ad campaign will fit in. Communicating the client's requirements and preferences to the creative and media departments and coordinating all activities related to the account are the responsibility of the account executive. The account coordinator or traffic manager is another vital member of the account services staff. This individual coordinates the work of all four departments throughout the advertising campaign, communicating timetables and monitoring progress.

A trainee in account services, the assistant account executive, usually has experience in advertising and a college degree. Entry-level duties might include handling inquires from clients and other departments, monitoring progress and deadlines in the creative department, communicating with the traffic manager on schedules and ad spots, and generally assisting the account executive. Advancement to account executive may occur after one or two successful years as an assistant. Initially account executives handle smaller accounts. They meet with clients to plan strategy and with other departments to see that it is implemented. They accept or reject ideas from the creative department, and they determine media and ad schedules according to the client's budget.

An assistant account executive who successfully handles ad campaigns and works effectively with clients should be promoted to senior account executive. Senior account executives work on larger accounts and may oversee and advise other account executives, thus gaining the opportunity to hone their administrative skills. The chief position in account services is that of the accounts supervisor or accounts manager. Managers not only oversee accounts but actively solicit new clients and advise and train sales staff. These managers are instrumental in bringing new business into the agency and assigning accounts to executives.

Acquiring and keeping accounts is what makes ad agencies profitable. It has been estimated that IBM spends between $400 and $500 million on ads each year (though an IBM insider claims the amount is actually half of that). When IBM decided to place all of its advertising with just one agency, Ogilvy & Mather, at least forty agencies worldwide lost large chunks of business. In turn, taking on IBM cost Ogilvy & Mather its other high-tech clients. Charlotte Beers, chairman of the agency and the highest-ranking woman in advertising, won the account by proposing a strategy she calls "brand stewardship" that involves analyzing the character of a brand in terms of the role it plays in the consumer's life. Ogilvy will collect reams of data from IBM's marketing executives to form an image for the company. Everyone in the advertising world is watching.

The Research Department

Information collected through consumer research and product testing is often the basis for an ad campaign because it identifies potential users of the product and why it should appeal to this particular market. The research department of an advertising agency functions very much like the marketing research department of any company, but the focus is, of course, on effective advertising. Monitoring trends is a vital function in that trends can determine how products are positioned. For example, the nation's divorce rate is edging lower as baby boomers reach middle age. For this reason more ads will probably focus on families using products.

An entry level job as a research project director usually requires a college or graduate degree and experience in advertising or marketing research. Research in an advertising agency means collecting information on how consumers perceive particular products. Conducting primary research involves the development of surveys that are usually conducted by outside firms and the analysis of survey results. Writing reports containing this analysis and additional information gathered from secondary sources such as the government or trade groups is the job of the project research director. These reports are used by account services, the creative department, and the media department in planning the advertising campaign. Once the campaign begins, research focuses on its effect on the intended audience and may recommend changes. Promotion to research account executive depends on talent and innovation. Devising new methods of product and market testing and recommending successful advertising strategies are sure ways to move up in the research department.

Years of successful experience should lead to the position of associate research director, then advertising research director, and finally research department manager. As in all departments in businesses, advancement involves taking on more supervisory and administrative duties. Administrative skills are universally useful, so movement from one department to another is not unusual, particularly for those with a background in research in which problem solving and data analysis are requisite skills.

The Creative Department

The largest number of advertising jobs are found in the creative department, which is composed of copywriters, graphic artists, and layout workers who work in teams under the art director and the copy chief. Figure 4.1 shows the structure of the creative department.

The creative team synthesizes information from the research department, the account executive, and the client to develop the advertisements that will

Figure 4.1 The Creative Department

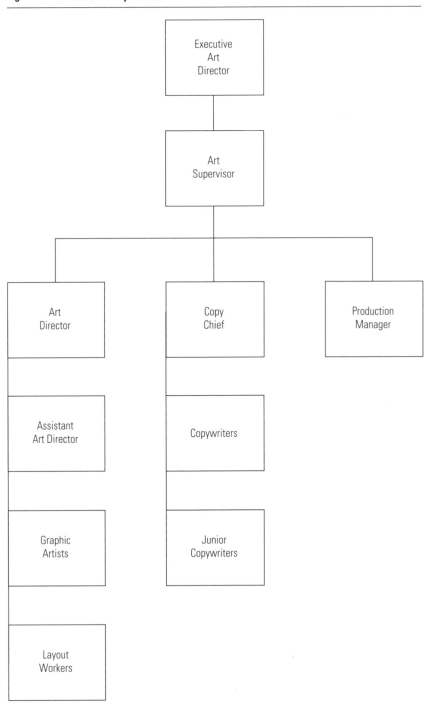

attract the targeted consumers to the client's product. Graphic designers and copywriters are essentially problem solvers, creating distinctive and innovative solutions to the problem of how best to attract and hold the attention of a specific group of people and persuade those people to buy what they are selling, whether it's a product, a service, or a statement of theology.

It is hard to capture the attention of today's magazine flipping, channel surfing public, so art directors are experimenting with every available tool including type. Letters now leap about ads and commercials, various typefaces are combined, sentences swim off in all directions. Computers make it easy to create special effects in type styles. Unfortunately, surveys point out that if the message is hard to read, consumers usually ignore it. U.S. agencies added the position of type director, used for years in Britain to solve this dilemma.

Most people think of advertising as catchy phrases and gimmicky slogans or jingles. Cleverness and originality are certainly a part of what is required for creative advertising professionals, and humor can be a very compelling sales tool. Small companies with small advertising budgets often ignore "political correctness" and rely on irreverence to sell their products. The article "In Your Face," appearing in the November 22, 1993 issue of *Forbes*, points out a few instances. For example, the ad for Rib Ticklers barbecue sauce features barnyard animals in a pastoral setting. In the background a lovely children's choir extols the virtue of these animals until a barbecue grill appears in the sky and the announcer says, "Hey! Here's an idea. Let's eat 'em!" Hooters countered criticism of their waitress uniforms with this spot featuring Rush Limbaugh—"Do you know that the shameless exploitation of women and animals is going on at the same time and the same place and you should stop it? Do the right thing. Go to Hooters and stop all this." The greatest public outcry is directed at beer and cigarette ads that appear to target children. Government and anti-smoking groups have criticized R.J. Reynolds Tobacco Company's Joe Camel, but the popular dromedary does sell cigarettes. Reynolds responded by featuring Danny Glover in public-service ads designed to discourage under-age smoking.

Ads may be designed to improve an image. In the General Motors Corporation campaign "Putting Quality on the Road," GM apologizes for past quality deficiencies and boasts about improvements. Sometimes advertising is used to change a product's image and reposition it. For example, one Hyundai ad campaign features its new sporty coupe to attract trendy upscale consumers. Xerox, which many consumers perceive as strictly a copier manufacturer due to strong brand identification, is using an ad campaign "Putting It Together" that focuses on document management. Its newest product, Xenith, can compute, scan, fax, copy—the ultimate in document-producing machines.

Companies often use celebrities to convey their advertising message both directly and indirectly. Consider the advertising value of having Andre Agassi win the U.S. Tennis Open wearing Nike products from head to toe. As part of their contracts, athletes are paid to wear company insignias or logos. Advertisers are capitalizing on the public's desire to identify with celebrities by using products they promote. Stars such as Michael Jordan, Shaquille O'Neal, Candice Bergen, and Bill Cosby are well compensated for helping a company sell its products. The soft-drink industry spends an annual average of $550 million on advertising, including advertisements featuring stars. An alternative approach in the underwear market is to replace stars with humorous commercials featuring regular guys caught in public in their underwear. The reason for the switch—everyone else is now using celebrity commercials. An important consideration in advertising is the target audience, that is, who does the buying. Marketing consultants suggest that the use of rugged sports stars and leading men is to appeal to women, who purchase about 55 to 60 percent of all men's underwear.

Laws to prevent misleading advertising only work some of the time. Like attorneys who slip in remarks that the judge orders the jury to disregard, companies often run misleading ads regardless of the lawsuits that follow. The Hot Rod Association took strong exception to an ad showing a monster truck rolling over five cars, crushing all but the Volvo. Volvo admitted reinforcing the roof of the car with lumber and steel for the stunt. Johnson & Johnson sued Bristol-Myers Squibb Co. over ads claiming Aspirin-Free Excedrin is more effective than Extra-Strength Tylenol when both products contain the same dose of the pain reliever acetaminophen. Because of required truth in advertising, Bristol-Myers has to prove its product's increased effectiveness. As more commercials attack competing products by name, maligned companies are charging that network review systems are allowing false ads on the air. Coca-Cola and Ford are among the most vocal and advocate hiring an independent panel of research experts to verify ad claims. Networks claim that their research executives are doing a good job and such a panel is unnecessary. Advertising industry ethics have been questioned in the past, and the problem of misleading advertising is unlikely to disappear, especially during hard economic times.

Normally a college degree and, even more important, a portfolio of writing samples and ideas are required for breaking into this highly competitive area. General knowledge of advertising trends and media is also required. Once hired as a junior copywriter, an individual might do everything from answering the telephone to taking part in creative brainstorming sessions. Creativity and the formation of ideas remain a mystery—a combination of knowledge and imagination that can be neither learned nor predicted. The ability to see things in new ways is vital in creative work.

A junior copywriter usually works under a copywriter for a training period. Once promoted to copywriter, one is responsible for writing ad copy, developing concepts for campaigns, and working with artists and layout workers to present finished ads and ideas for commercials. These artists and layout personnel work under an art director to create the visual impact of the ad by selecting photographs, drawing illustrations, choosing print size and type, or sketching scenes for commercials. In addition to preparing magazine and television layouts, they also design packages and create corporate logos, trademarks, and symbols. Production managers oversee the actual printing of ads, filming of commercials, or recording of radio spots. Promotions to senior copywriter and then to copy chief are contingent on talent and success. Producing good ads that sell products and make clients happy count more than years of experience. Like sales, what you produce forms the basis for how you are evaluated. Senior copywriters work on projects for the large national accounts that increase the agency's reputation and profits. Copy chiefs supervise other copywriters and work closely with media and account executives in developing ad campaign strategies.

The Media Department

Once ads are created, they are placed in media selected for the broadest impact. Media professionals develop a media strategy or the proper media mix for best promoting the product. This involves defining the target audience, where they live, and how they can best be reached. Using information from the research department and computers, media planners try to reach the largest number of potential customers in the most cost-effective way.

The new technology only partly explains the movement away from ads delivered to undifferentiated audiences via broadcast television networks and mass circulation magazines and newspapers. The decline in both broadcast network viewing and publications subscriptions combined with rising ad prices has caused marketers to examine alternate media like cable television and the thousands of new special interest publications that have arisen in the last ten years. Basic cable networks offer a highly targeted, often upscale, audience to advertisers at lower rates than the major networks. Regional sports cable networks have been big advertising winners, with ad revenues rising roughly 35 percent per year.

Marketers have concluded that targeted messages through specialized media are economical and effective. Advertisers want ads addressed to age, income, psychology, and buying patterns placed in media that target specific groups. The desired media packages include combinations of magazines, television programs, books, and videotapes. Technology has produced still other advertising media. Sony Corporation has erected a 23 1/2-by-32-foot outdoor color video display in Times Square in New York City, showing ads including spots for Sony's CBS Records and Columbia Pictures as well as news and public service announcements. Prodigy, the videotext service developed by Sears and IBM, runs ads along with its information. In-store advertising in groceries has gone from ads on fliers, shopping carts, and checkout dividers to television sets mounted over the checkout counter running various ads. Thus the field of media planning is becoming more complex and challenging.

Candidates for positions in media planning are chosen for their numeric and analytic skills as well as the ability to accept high levels of responsibility. College graduates enter the media department as assistant media planners. Working under experienced planners, beginners are involved in computation and analysis of numbers provided by research or audience ratings done by outside sources such as Nielsen. Advancement to the position of media planner brings far more responsibility. Media planners work close-ly with account services and sometimes directly with clients in determining the best media mix, that is, how much television, magazine, or other cover-age to use. Choosing from many options makes this a challenging job. Adding to the challenge is the need to adhere to the client's media budget, although the media group can make recommendations regarding budget.

Once a media plan is accepted by the client, media professionals begin meeting with advertising sales representatives from various media and eval-uating their proposals. Negotiating contracts for advertising space or air time according to the media plan is the next step. This may be done by media di-rectors and their associates or, in larger agencies, regional or national spot buyers skilled in negotiating with sales representatives of mass media. After five to ten years of experience, media directors can advance to media plan-ners. The media manager, who is in charge of both planning and buying, holds the top job in media.

Media sales reps usually enter the field from positions in media planning, sometimes as spot buyers. Most work on straight or part commission and, therefore, have considerable earning potential. Media sales is high-pressure work. A recent *Wall Street Journal* article on stress in the workplace cited an instance in which an ad salesman screamed so loudly in an argument with his boss that he ruptured a lung. Though this is an extreme example, certain jobs can be stressful and must be evaluated as such by prospective job seek-ers. Positions in sales are discussed in chapters 6 and 7.

Along with strong quantitative skills, media professionals must also pos-sess strong communications and interpersonal skills. Functioning as part of a team and acquiescing to clients' wishes and directives from account services require an ability to work well with others and a willingness to compromise. The cost of media is the big-budget item in advertising. Consequently, the pressures and demands on the media department are great. However, media is an excellent avenue into account services.

TYPES OF SALES PROMOTION

Three types of sales promotion contribute to the overall promotion effort: trade promotions, sales force promotions, and consumer promotions. Trade promotions are geared toward intermediaries such as retailers. Manufactur-ers motivate intermediaries to carry their products by offering such incen-tives as free goods, dealer sales contests, trade show appearances, and paid cooperative ads. Both manufacturers and retailers offer sales force promo-tions including sales meetings, contests, and bonuses. The final push to sell the product is through consumer promotions, which include samples, coupons, trading stamps, rebates, point-of-purchase displays, exhibits, brochures, catalogs, sweepstakes, contests, and free gift-with-purchase. Shampoo with free conditioner, prizes inside cereal boxes, plastic dishes with the dog food—all of these motivate consumers to buy certain products. Low-cost marketing tools such as matchbooks, magnets, and swizzle sticks function as miniature billboards. For example, Stir-it, one of the largest producers of stirrers, sells four billion sticks a year to airlines, casinos, hotels, companies, and restaurant chains—700 million coffee stirrers to McDonald's alone—at a cost of from one to four cents a stick depending on design. A simple concept like the swizzle stick lends itself to clever product promotion. In a ski-resort promotion a couple of years ago, Heublein gave away vodka cocktails with swizzle sticks designed with logoed tops that could be broken off and used as pins on sweaters or caps.

The up-beat, try-it-you'll-like-it tone of sales promotion helps to launch new products. A company must succeed in motivating consumers to try its product before it can be market tested. If testing reveals that the product is well received, the company may want to intensify promotion efforts to ensure that it has a winner. The power of promotion efforts and their importance to the success of products cannot be overestimated. Unless the company can stimulate consumers to try new products, even the ones with the best potential are destined to fail because, in business, bottom-line profits determine which products remain on store shelves.

POSITIONS IN SALES PROMOTION

Much of what was written about advertising is also true for sales promotion, and many positions are similar. Sales promotion professionals may work for manufacturers, wholesalers, retailers, or sales promotion houses that operate roughly the same way as advertising agencies. A sales promotion specialist may play a role in product development, both learning about the product and suggesting ways to launch it. Sales promotion is highly specialized and not for beginners. Because of its importance and cost, sales promotion professionals enter the field with considerable knowledge in graphic arts, technical tools, and marketing. Most commonly, sales promotion professionals have had experience in either advertising or sales prior to entering the field.

Creativity is important in designing sales promotion campaigns. Coming up with something new and catchy that attracts consumers to the product is a challenge in a consumer society constantly bombarded by new products and promises. Demonstrators and models show the product to the public in shopping malls, grocery stores, and at trade shows. Graphic artists and copywriters work together to produce packaging for samples, coupons, buttons, T-shirts, and other promotion items. Layouts, materials, sizes, and shapes are all part of the creative process. Sales promotion efforts are planned and coordinated by a specialist assigned to the product.

Just as an account executive works with a client in an advertising agency, a sales promotion specialist provides the same services. Considering a client's product, sales promotion budget, and marketing research collected both for the product and similar products, a sales promotion specialist plans a campaign and directs a creative team in producing items needed to carry it out. A good specialist possesses research abilities, administrative skills, and creativity.

OPPORTUNITIES FOR ADVERTISING AND SALES PROMOTION PROFESSIONALS

Faster-than-average growth in advertising agencies is anticipated in the future because of intense competition both in domestic and global markets. Such competition requires companies to strengthen marketing and promotion efforts. Primary growth will be in overseas markets. Contributing to this growth are increasing worldwide acceptance of the General Agreements on Tariffs and Trade (GATT). These agreements are expected to lead to the founding of the World Trade Organization (WTO), which is designed to remove physical and technical barriers to trade by standardizing health, safety, and other technical requirements. Thus, products meeting WTO specifications will be automatically approved for sale from country to country, increasing global marketing opportunities.

A decade ago megamergers among advertising agencies resulted in twenty "superagencies," half of which are controlled by five holding companies. At the time, all these agencies offered comprehensive services often including sophisticated marketing research and in-house production facilities to clients and on a global scale. The result was that some divisions weren't as profitable as expected and the large agencies acquired a lot of debt. The 1990s trend is for agencies to delayer their managements and unbundle their services to compete with the up-coming, midsize agencies who are winning more and more customers. These smaller firms are willing to negotiate their commissions and are often more flexible in their approach to satisfying their customers needs. Most of the top U.S. agencies are headquartered in New York City and maintain satellite offices around the world.

In Canada, almost every major global agency has an office in Toronto. Advertising and sales promotion in Canada differs from U.S. work in both magnitude and style. With a population only 10 percent the size of the U.S. population, agency accounts are considerably smaller. More specific government restrictions limit what can be said on broadcast media about both products being offered and their competitors. Those seeking employment in Canada should be fluent in both English and French. A free booklet entitled "So You Want to Be in an Advertising Agency" can be obtained by writing

Institute for Canadian Advertising
30 Soudan Avenue
Toronto, Ontario M4S 1V6

Although demand is strong for advertising and sales promotion executives, the new graduate enters a highly competitive job market. A survey of college educators and advertising agency recruiters suggests that college preparation for entry-level jobs is oriented toward the development of job-specific attributes gained through courses in advertising, journalism, and business. Recruiters today, however, are looking for students with skills in advertising coupled with courses in areas such as history, humanities, and anthropology. Tomorrow's advertising graduates must be prepared to enter a competitive global environment that will require a broader perspective.

Although U.S. Department of Labor projections for 2000 suggest growth in employment at over 30 percent for marketing research analysts, advertising managers, and visual artists, employers are likely to be highly selective. The most motivated, energetic, well-organized candidates with top-notch analytic and communications skills will land the best jobs.

Salaries in ad agencies and in corporate advertising departments are fairly close for the same positions today, but predictions are that agency pay increases might slightly exceed those in corporate marketing departments in the future. Ad agencies and marketing personnel work closely together and a huge salary difference could cause problems in these working relationships. It isn't unusual for advertising and sales promotion professionals to move from corporate to agency settings and vice versa. Agency executive compensation levels are often tied to the size of the agency's billings, while corporate executive compensation varies with performance-tied bonuses. In general, entry-level salaries throughout the advertising industry are low, averaging about $14,000 to $25,000. This is partly a function of supply and demand, where highly qualified candidates encounter stiff competition for existing jobs. The training and experience gained by beginners, however, enables them to more effectively compete for jobs higher up the ladder. Salaries increase considerably with advancement. The following salaries for both agencies and marketers are rough approximations; actual salaries are contingent on experience, job duties, and the size and prestige of the employer.

Figure 4.2 Salaries for Agencies and Marketers

Agency Title	Salary
CEO	$140,000–$151,000
Creative director	$95,000–$102,000
Art director	$52,000–$55,000
Chief copywriter	$52,000–$55,000
Media director	$55,000–$59,000
Senior account executive	$69,000–$74,000
Account executive	$42,000–$45,000
Assistant account executive	$20,000–40,000
Media planner	$20,000–27,000
Media supervisor	$25,000–55,000
Traffic manager	$18,000–20,000
Marketing research project director	$30,000–55,000
Junior copywriter	$14,000–18,000
Copywriter	$20,000–40,000
Assistant art director	$14,000–18,000

Salaries for most positions are similar in non-agency settings. For executives, the average base salary for the vice-president of marketing in all size companies ranges from $127,000-$133,000 and for the vice-president of advertising from $100,000-$107,000.

SOURCES OF INFORMATION

Numerous books and periodicals about advertising and sales promotion are available. Of all career areas in marketing, these fields are described in the most detail. In addition, trade associations offer much general information on the field and professional development. Below is a partial list of resources.

Publications

Two popular advertising periodicals are *Advertising Age* and *Brandweek*, weekly publications found in most public and college libraries. There are dozens of excellent periodicals for advertising professionals. Those interested in media can read *Broadcast Week* and *Marketing and Media Decisions*. Job seekers can use directories such as *Roster and Organization of the American Association of Advertising Agencies* and *Standard Directory of Advertising Agencies*.

Associations

Some associations for advertising and sales promotion professionals that offer information are listed below. Some offer student memberships at a discounted rate.

> The Advertising Club of New York
> 235 Park Avenue South, Sixth floor
> New York, NY 10003
> (212)533-8080
> > (This organization has a Young Professionals Division for professionals under 30 or with less than two years of experience.)

> The Advertising Council
> 261 Madison Avenue
> New York, NY 10016-2303
> (212)922-1500

> Advertising Research Foundation
> 641 Lexington Avenue
> New York, NY 10022
> (212)751-5656

> American Advertising Federation
> 1101 Vermont Avenue Northwest, Suite 500
> Washington, DC 20005
> (202)898-0089

American Association of Advertising Agencies
666 Third Avenue, Thirteenth Floor
New York, NY 10017
(212)682-2500

Copywriter's Council of America
Communications Building 102
7 Putter Lane, Box 102
Middle Island, NY 11953-0102
(516)924-8555

The Council of Sales Promotion Agencies
750 Summer Street, Second Floor
Stamford, CT 06901
(203)325-3911

Promotion Industry Club
1805 North Mill Street, Suite A
Naperville, IL 60563
(708)369-3772

Promotion Marketing Association of America
257 Park Avenue, Eleventh Floor
New York, NY 10001
(212)206-1100

Radio Advertising Bureau
304 Park Avenue South
New York, NY 10010
(212)387-2100

Retail Advertising and Marketing Association, International
500 North Michigan Avenue, Suite 600
Chicago, IL 60611
(312)245-9011

Television Bureau of Advertising
850 3rd Avenue, Tenth Floor
New York, NY 10022
(212)486-1111

Internships

The American Advertising Federation listed above is an excellent source of information on advertising internships offered by many of its members. A membership list may be obtained by writing to the organization. Although all companies listed do not sponsor interns, many do. Internships in advertising are offered during summer, winter recesses, and regular school terms. Not all interns receive pay; those who do earn on average $200 to $300 per week. Because internships are such a desirable way to break into the field of advertising, applicants face stiff competition. It is, therefore, recommended that applicants develop a good resume, target an area of specialization in which they would like to work, and use all available resources to get leads on internships.

InterAd

Twice a year the American Graduate School in International Management holds InterAd competitions in which student teams create complete marketing and advertising campaigns for launching real products into international markets. Corporate sponsors make donations to cover research costs and production materials. These sponsors often incorporate InterAd campaign elements into their international marketing plans.

The competition is judged by advertising agency and marketing executives from around the country who then may interview students of the competing teams for jobs. Many young advertising professionals launch their careers through participation in the InterAd competition. The students gain experience in international marketing that is invaluable because this arena will afford many new opportunities to advertising professionals in the future.

The InterAd competition is open to students from schools across the country. The American Graduate School of International Management itself offers a program of study to those students specifically interested in international business. It requires from twelve to eighteen months to complete the master of international management program. More information on international marketing is covered in chapter 9.

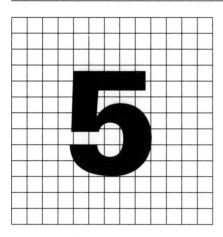

CAREERS IN PUBLIC RELATIONS AND CUSTOMER SERVICE

Low prices and profit margins, the high cost of implementing new technology, better educated and more price-conscious consumers, and expensive advertising and sales promotion make the use of public relations and customer service more vital to the success of the company. Any good business person knows that it costs a lot less to retain old customers than to acquire new ones. Building relationships is the way to keep customers loyal. Public relations (PR) is the means to build a positive relationship with the community and customer service is the way to foster a long-term relationship with the individual customer.

THE ROLE OF PUBLIC RELATIONS IN PROMOTION

Public relations involves the creation of publicity. Publicity is information about the company and its products that appears in the mass media; it falls into the category of news. Unlike paid advertising, publicity may be good or bad; it may originate with the company or the media; and it is aired free.

Organizations today depend on goodwill not only from consumers who make up the markets for their products but from the public at large. The actions of an organization in producing and marketing a product sometimes have a wide impact. Therefore, public relations professionals must understand attitudes and concerns of various groups such as government agencies, environmentalists, consumer advocates, stockholders, and residents of communities in which companies build their plants.

Lobbying for favorable legislation and against unfavorable legislation is one of PR's numerous activities. Monitoring and advising management of societal changes that could affect future actions of the firm is another. The basic mission of PR is building, maintaining, and improving the public image of the firm. A positive public image helps to promote the company's products. Because of the national attention to worthwhile causes in the 1990s, many companies are engaging in cause marketing. Magazine companies are helping to sponsor and publicize fund-raising events for causes such as shelters for the homeless, AIDS prevention and cure, and breast cancer research.

THE NATURE OF PUBLIC RELATIONS WORK

Entry-level work as an assistant account executive in public relations includes acquiring information from a variety of sources and maintaining files, a fundamental part of the research process. With experience, PR professionals begin to write press releases, executives' speeches, and articles for both internal and external publications. Other duties such as working with media contacts, planning special events, and making travel arrangements for prominent people are all part of PR.

Promotion to public relations account executive depends on the demonstrated ability to generate innovative ideas, to work well with others, and to communicate effectively with groups of employees, media representatives, and clients. Once promoted to account executive, the professional works independently and directly with clients, planning and executing a public relations campaign strategy. Advancement to public relations account supervisor carries with it the responsibility over major campaigns and the budgets for groups of accounts. The director of account services in a public relations firm, often an owner or partner, typically oversees campaigns and budgets and works to attract new clients.

Public relations, like advertising and sales promotion, is campaign oriented. When a campaign is launched, it is often necessary to work overtime. Meals with clients and travel are sometimes on the agenda. Deadlines and pressures are implicit in this type of work. A small group of PR professionals even specialize in restoring battered images of celebrities at rates that can reach $2,500 per month per client. The satisfaction derived from creatively planning a campaign and enjoying its success is worth the irregular hours and extra demands for those with the proper temperament and disposition for PR work.

OPPORTUNITIES IN PUBLIC RELATIONS

The public relations industry has experienced little overall growth in the past year. The growth that occurred in public relations firms due to increased billings was offset by downsizing in the corporate sector. Public relations professionals are hired by businesses, nonprofit organizations, trade associations, government agencies, colleges, prominent individuals, large advertising agencies with PR departments, and public relations firms that serve a wide range of clients. Although some public relations agencies are large, most employ fewer than a dozen people. Agencies located in smaller cities are projected to offer some of the best job opportunities in the future. In Canada, major agencies are located in the large population centers of Ontario and Quebec. In general, because of the size of Canadian markets, both projects and budgets will be smaller than in the U.S. Bilingual applicants are given preference.

Public relations firms and professionals may specialize in any of a number of areas:

- *Consumer affairs*, in which PR professionals field inquiries from customers, prepare educational materials, address consumer safety and quality issues
- *Government relations*, which involves lobbying for or against certain legislation, researching and presenting information to the staff of government agencies, recommending legislation useful to the company
- *Investor relations*, in which the PR professional serves as a liaison between the shareholders and the company, preparing reports, planning meetings, handling shareholder inquiries, and encouraging investment
- *Employee relations*, where the PR professional coordinates communication between employees and management by producing in-house publications and arranging meetings, seminars, and conferences
- *Community relations*, which involves organizing programs, activities, tours, classes, and publications for schools, civic groups, neighborhood associations, and interested individuals
- *International relations*, in which responsibilities include researching foreign customs, preparing information to be used in foreign countries, entertaining foreign visitors, and introducing the company abroad
- *Media relations*, which requires writing and placing press releases, producing clips for television, organizing press conferences, and arranging appearances of company executives

The type and amount of public relations effort in any of these areas depends on the size and nature of the organization. In-house PR is normally done by a small staff working under the director of public relations. Larger firms may have two PR departments—one for internal company PR and one for product promotion. In PR firms, the number of employees and their titles depend on the size of the firm. Like advertising, good PR work begins with research to determine a client's goals and how best to accomplish these goals in light of the competition. This is true whether a client is a business or a political candidate. The areas above have many activities in common that typify public relations work: research, writing, media placement, public speaking, and event coordination.

EDUCATION REQUIREMENTS

Persuasive individuals who have excellent verbal and written communications skills and hold a college degree may successfully enter the field of public relations. Applicants hold degrees in a variety of areas—communications, business, and liberal arts, among others. Competition for PR jobs is keen, and individuals with strong communications or journalism backgrounds have an edge. Most colleges offer programs in public relations through the communications department. This is also true of advertising programs because of the creative and media aspects of the jobs.

Salaries

Salaries in public relations positions vary according to experience, geography, industry, and area of specialization. Men tend to earn more than women with the same number of years of experience, but there are signs that the gender gap is narrowing. Typically, each five years of experience yields $10,000 more in salary. Salaries are highest in the East, followed by the Midwest, West, with lowest salaries in the South. Large corporations tend to pay the highest salaries. The following table of median salaries was developed from information in the *Public Relations Journal*, July 1993 issue.

Figure 5.1 Median Salaries by Title and Type of Organization

Title	Type of Organization		
	PR firm	Corporation	Government/Health Care/Non-profit
Account execs	$29,016	$35,715	$29,677
Supervisors	$49,877	$55,480	$42,716
Senior management	$66,467	$62,613	$68,468

Salaries are higher in certain areas of specialization in public relations than in others. These areas are ranked from highest median salaries to lowest in Figure 5.2.

Figure 5.2 Areas of Specialization Ranked by Median Salary

1. Investor relations	$66,707
2. International	62,240
3. Environmental affairs	54,920
4. Government relations	54,595
5. Issues management	54,458
6. Crisis management	52,508
7. Public affairs	51,926
8. Technology	50,718
9. Corporate communications	50,634
10. Strategic planning	50,547

11. Generalists	49,108
12. Research	47,763
13. Media relations	46,765
14. Employee relations	46,142
15. Community relations	45,445
16. Marketing	45,345
17. Special events	45,224
18. Publicity	44,893
19. Public relations education	43,674
20. Advertising	43,416

Finally, Figure 5.3 ranks industries in terms of median salary.

Figure 5.3 Industries Ranked by Median Salary

1. Industrial/manufacturing	$62,303
2. Public relations counseling firm	53,728
3. Utility	52,672
4. Financial/insurance	49,602
5. Media/communications	49,473
6. Miscellaneous services	47,915
7. Scientific/technical	44,351
8. Government	44,019
9. Association/foundation	43,388
10. Solo practitioner	43,101
11. Transportation/hotels/ resorts/entertainment	41,843
12. Health care	41,550
13. Advertising agency	41,066
14. Education	41,008

Because of keen competition, those interested in PR work should try to get some meaningful experience prior to college graduation. Work experience and knowledge in an area of specialization or a specific industry are very helpful. Internships during college or as a first job after graduation provide an excellent way of gaining experience. Employers use interns' skill levels to screen them for potential entry-level hiring. Because of the importance of internships and the competitive nature of the job market, many colleges and universities require internships for graduation. Job applicants should prepare a portfolio of PR projects on which they have worked. The college campus affords many opportunities for involvement in such projects, such as joining the staff of the campus newspaper, radio, or television station or becoming active in student activities programs. Working as a volunteer on political campaigns is also excellent experience.

SOURCES OF PUBLIC RELATIONS INFORMATION

Internships in public relations are available but are not easy to get. Professional public relations associations sometimes sponsor internships and know of opportunities for beginners. A Career Press publication, *Public Relations Career Directory*, contains articles, job-finding information, and entry-level openings in the U.S. and Canada.

Associations such as the ones listed below enable PR professionals to share information, take part in seminars and conferences, and remain up-to-date on trends that impact their careers.

Institute for Public Relations Research and Education
3800 South Tamiami Trail, Suite N
Sarasota, FL 34239
(813)955-5577

International Association of Business Communicators
1 Hallidie Plaza, Suite 600
San Francisco, CA 94102
(415)433-3400

National Investor Relations Institute
200 L Street N.W., Suite 701
Washington, DC 20036
(202)861-0630

Public Affairs Council
1019 19th Street N.W., Suite 200
Washington, DC 20036
(202)872-1790

Public Relations Society of America
33 Irving Place, Third floor
New York, NY 10003-2376
(212)995-2230
    (This organization has a student branch—Public Relations
    Student Society of America at the address above, (212)460-
    1474.)

Women in Communications, Inc.
2101 Wilson Boulevard, Suite 417
Arlington, VA 22201
(703)528-4200

Public relations periodicals offer a wealth of information regarding the current happenings in the field and advice to professionals. Job openings are also published in the classified ad sections of various publications such as *Public Relations Journal*, *Public Relations Quarterly*, *Publicist*, *Public Relations News*, *Public Relations Review*, and *PR Reporter*. Some or all of these can be found in public or university libraries.

THE IMPORTANCE OF CUSTOMER SERVICE IN TODAY'S ECONOMY

We live in a service-oriented economy. Even when selling goods rather than services, courteous and helpful customer service adds value to the product and contributes significantly to customer satisfaction. Today's marketers realize that it is far less expensive to maintain a current customer than to find a new one. For this reason, most companies are attempting to build long-term customer relationships. Satisfied car buyers tend to buy the same brand over and over. This can add up to several hundred thousand dollars over the span of a lifetime.

Given that one never gets a second chance to make a first impression, sales personnel are being retrained to think in terms of customer service. Providing the kind of useful information and helping customers make intelligent choices in terms of their individual needs and values is the current orientation to sales and customer retention. In business-to-business marketing, suppliers are in effect entering partnerships with customers by helping them to improve processes, reduce costs, and deliver quality. Successful customers buy more products from their suppliers.

Global competition, technological change, and shifting customer demands place pressure on companies to retrain their personnel to function in a dynamic new marketplace. Using the new technology and focusing more on solving customers' problems are at the heart of this retraining. To retain a customer base, companies must find out from customers what their needs are and how well they are being met and design products and services accordingly. Another key is employee retention. Experienced employees better understand what customers need, and satisfied employees help customers buy more.

Smart companies respond to customer complaints with a prompt personal reply sometimes accompanied by coupons and free products. Customer complaints can be a valuable source of information for product development. Sincere responses to complaints and follow-up corrective action can generate positive word-of-mouth advertising.

Adding value to products and services by providing better customer service is an effective competitive strategy for every company. Some ways to add value include learning a customer's business and suggesting new ways to improve it, providing a guarantee, offering some free service, and providing a customer with options.

CUSTOMER SERVICE SALES

Customer service is everybody's job—sales personnel; support staff who handle orders and problems; distribution personnel; and managers who assess customer needs, plan products to satisfy them, and train and maintain satisfied employees. The position of customer service representative exists in many companies. Customer service reps have been around for a long time. We speak to them to set up accounts for banking, cable television, and utilities. These representatives deliver the company's product or service to its customers. They provide information, answer questions, and help customers as do other sales personnel. In addition, they are troubleshooters who handle complaints, expedite repairs and maintenance, and explain warranties. These positions require courtesy, helpfulness, competence, and product knowledge. In the past, customer service was considered an area that supported sales. In today's service-oriented economy, this rapidly growing field has been accurately renamed —customer service sales.

Roughly 75 percent of all jobs in the U.S. are in a service industry. Customer service sales personnel include stock brokers, travel agents, insurance agents, real estate agents, property appraisers, health club operators, and owners of beauty salons, day care centers, and housekeeping services—to mention only a few. All of these individuals are selling services. Many positions require the use of computers and knowledge of industry-specific software. All require excellent communications and marketing skills.

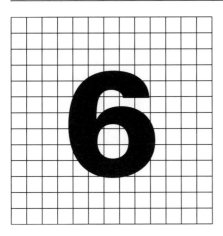

CAREERS IN INDUSTRIAL, WHOLESALE, AND DIRECT SALES

The 1990s are witnessing a metamorphosis from the in-your-face salesperson to the "relationship manager." Though successful sales personnel require many of the same attributes as in former years, they require a few more plus a new orientation. Solving problems and satisfying customers as well as generating sales volume are measures of success. Some companies have begun to tie salary to customer satisfaction and to eliminate commissions in favor of bonuses based on corporate profits. This sales approach requires more training, knowledge, and teamwork than in previous years. Computer companies such as IBM and pharmaceutical companies such as Merck & Company, Inc. both use this approach.

Sales is a vital part of the marketing function. Sales professionals have a key role in moving products into the marketplace. After production, manufacturers may opt for any or all of the available channels of distribution by selling products directly to customers, to retailers, or to wholesale intermediaries. The area of wholesaling is unfamiliar to most consumers who deal only with retailers. Wholesaling is the link between the manufacturer and the retailer who sells to consumers. Basically, wholesalers sell to everybody except ultimate consumers—including retailers, other wholesalers, and manufacturers. Although manufacturers may sell their merchandise directly to retailers, wholesaling intermediaries provide many valuable services both to their suppliers (manufacturers) and to their customers (retailers). Often it is more cost effective for a manufacturer to sell goods at a reduced price through wholesalers who incur the costs of sales personnel and warehouse expenses. Manufacturers who sell directly to final consumers often use the services of self-employed manufacturers' representatives.

A growing trend is direct marketing. This term refers to a variety of methods of nonstore selling, including direct selling, direct response retailing, database marketing, direct mail, and telemarketing. Direct marketing may be done by manufacturers or retailers. This chapter focuses on careers in sales for those interested in employment by manufacturers, wholesalers, and direct marketers. Careers in retail stores will be discussed in the following chapter.

THE SALES PROFESSIONAL

Regardless of employer or type of sales (industrial, wholesale, retail, or direct), all sales professionals perform similar functions. Selling can be hard work with long and irregular working hours, extensive travel and entertaining, and sometimes reluctant and unwilling customers. Sales representatives must possess self-confidence, persistence, and optimism. Excellent communications skills are essential because sales representatives are also expected to be technical advisors, educators, and trainers. Persuading potential customers that a product will best solve their problems and satisfy their needs is part of the art of selling. People buy benefits, not products, and salespeople need to sell solutions. People want clean carpets, not vacuum cleaners; peace of mind, not insurance; happy children, not toys. Therefore, to sell a vacuum cleaner, insurance, or any other product, a sales rep must persuade the potential customer that this product is the best on the market to satisfy the customer's needs.

The hard sell is definitely out of vogue. The effective salesperson today helps the customer to buy. This is done through first asking questions to better understand the customer's wants and needs and second, providing information that helps clarify these needs. Then, while making recommendations, the sales rep talks about company products and their advantages to the customer. The emphasis remains on the customer. Customer service is the concept behind successful selling. Sales requires individuals who are genuinely interested in their customers, want to see them happy with their choices, and can effectively communicate this desire. Sales representatives are selling themselves and their companies, not merely products. This is how they generate repeat business. They are gaining customers, not merely making one-time sales.

THE NATURE OF SALES WORK

Sales representatives perform numerous activities, including some of the following:

1. Setting goals, planning, and making schedules.
2. Identifying and contacting prospective customers.
3. Maintaining contacts with current customers and anticipating their needs.
4. Planning and making sales presentations.
5. Reviewing sales orders, scheduling delivery dates, and handling special details.

6. Maintaining up-to-date records and reports.
7. Handling complaints and problems.
8. Monitoring the competition.
9. Learning new product information and marketing strategies.
10. Evaluating price trends and advising customers.

Time management is crucial to successful selling. Sales representatives must carefully allocate their time among the above activities. Some industries have cycles with peak selling periods during which more time must be spent on customer contact. Slack periods provide time for record keeping, follow-up with customers, researching new products, and so forth. Figure 6.1 lists the steps in the selling process.

Figure 6.1 The Personal Selling Process

✔ Step 1: Prospecting

✔ Step 2: Preparing the pre-approach

✔ Step 3: Approaching the prospect

✔ Step 4: Making the sales presentation

✔ Step 5: Handling objections

✔ Step 6: Closing the sale

✔ Step 7: Follow up

Today sales representatives use technology to make their jobs easier. Sales automation is a $1 billion industry. It is predicted that revenues will exceed $2.7 billion by 1997. Prices of laptops and notebooks are decreasing, making them affordable for more and more sales representatives. Personal computers and notebooks aid in record keeping and information gathering. Car and cellular telephones save time. Fax machines and communications networks get information to customers and the home office quickly. Using technology is essential for sales professionals to compete in the marketplace of today.

A college degree in marketing or an industry-related area is preferred for many positions in sales, but not always necessary. However, promotions to company manager usually go to degree holders. The professional association Sales and Marketing Executives International (SMEI) offers a certification program for sales and marketing managers. The SMEI Accreditation Institute verifies educational experience, knowledge, and standards of conduct of candidates for certification.

INDUSTRIAL SALES AND WHOLESALING

Computers and communications networks are having a major impact on the relationship between suppliers and buyers. Computer links between suppliers and targeted consumers are beginning to eliminate the need for some inter-mediaries. However, database technology has helped retailers and whole-salers alike to determine exactly what products are needed and when. The stocking practices of both have become more efficient and less wasteful. Consider Tech Data, a computer supplies wholesaler who buys 14,000 prod-ucts from 300 manufacturers and sells them to 45,000 customers. In the com-puter industry, where items become obsolete very quickly, these products must be sold immediately. Tech Data uses a mainframe computer that can process 250 transactions per second and a personal computer equipped with a fax modem on every sales representative's desk to accomplish this.

Various opportunities and work environments exist for those in industrial sales and wholesaling. Sales representatives may be employed by manufac-turers or merchant wholesalers, or they may be self-employed as manufac-turers' agents or wholesale dealers.

Company Sales Representatives and Managers

Sales representatives employed by companies are given training and expense accounts. Depending on the company's products, they may sell to whole-salers, retailers, directly to industrial users, or to individuals through manu-facturer's outlet stores. Inside sales workers stay in an office and solicit or take orders by phone. In addition, they process orders and monitor inventory. Field sales workers visit customers to solicit sales, provide information on new products, or to render technical assistance. Some sales representatives offer services to retailers such as checking and reordering stock or suggest-ing promotion and display techniques. Industrial or electronic equipment sales representatives may install and service what they sell. Sales representa-tives work with purchasing agents and other buyers for customer companies.

In large companies, sales representatives work under a district manager and, if promoted, may hold that position themselves. Levels of management within companies differ according to the organization's size and structure, but most sales representatives work under a sales manager. The sales manag-er establishes training programs, assigns territories, and defines goals for the sales representatives. The ability of sales managers to train and develop oth-ers is one key to their success and subsequent promotion. District sales man-agers may work under product or brand managers, depending on the company and its product offerings. Sales managers get information from dealers and distributors on customer preferences. In addition, they project future sales and inventory requirements for the geographical area to which they are assigned. The district sales manager reports to the regional sales manager, who reports to the national sales manager, who works directly with the vice-president of marketing. Not all sales representatives aspire to climb the corporate ladder, preferring the autonomy of sales work to the headaches of management. It is not unusual for effective sales representatives on com-mission to earn more than managers whose salaries are fixed.

Purchasing Agents   Companies usually employ purchasing agents to obtain items they need for production. Purchasing agents are also employed by local, state, or federal governments. Normally specializing in one product or group of products, they shop for the best quality at the lowest price. Purchasing agents arrange payment and delivery of products according to their employer's specifications. They may deal with company sales representatives, manufacturers' agents, or wholesale intermediaries.

As a field, purchasing is becoming more complex. Those interested in purchasing as a career should study topics such as negotiation, purchasing law, international purchasing, federal regulations, computerized purchasing, and product liability. There is a need for more purchasing programs in schools across a broader geographical area. Well-trained purchasing professionals are in demand.

Manufacturers' Agents   Manufacturers' agents or representatives are independent business people who may sell one product, a group of similar products, or a variety of products to different types of customers. Normally they are assigned a territory in which only they can sell the company's products. The manufacturer pays a commission for each sale. Manufacturers' representatives have no expense accounts or company benefits as do company-employed sales representatives. What they do have is total freedom—the advantage of being self-employed. Manufacturer's representatives are seasoned sellers, not beginners. The best preparation for obtaining permission from a company to sell its products is to first gain experience by working as a company-employed salesperson within the industry. Once accepted as a manufacturer's representative, an agent provides an invaluable service to manufacturers who cannot afford to maintain a company sales force. The manufacturer pays a commission only on products sold, but ambitious agents can earn sizable salaries if they are excellent sales people.

Merchant Wholesalers   About 80 percent of wholesaling establishments, accounting for slightly over half of wholesale sales, are classified as merchant wholesalers. These independently owned businesses purchase products from the manufacturers and resell them to other manufacturers, wholesalers, or retailers. Usually referred to simply as wholesalers, those specializing in industrial products are often called industrial distributors, and those specializing in consumer products are called jobbers. Wholesalers may provide a range of services, including ordering, shipping, warehousing, and credit. They may stock a variety of products, one or two product lines, or, in the case of specialty wholesalers, part of one product line.

Wholesale Dealer

Basically, the job of wholesale dealers, also called merchandise brokers, is to bring buyers and sellers together. These dealers or brokers may work for either the buyer or the seller. Whoever employs them pays the commission. Typically, wholesale dealers will find the products specified by their client companies at the best price, add their commission (roughly 30 percent), and give the customer the quote. Although the dealer may negotiate deals on behalf of the client, the client decides whether to accept or reject these deals. If employed by manufacturers, the dealers will find a customer for the manufacturers' products and negotiate a deal. Brokers handle both goods and services. Most individuals have dealt with real estate, insurance, or investment brokers.

Other Wholesalers

Numerous other types of wholesalers provide similar wholesaling services as well as career opportunities for those interested in wholesale sales. Included are petroleum bulk plants and terminals, which resell petroleum products to industrial users, retailers, and other wholesalers. Farm product assemblers buy grain, cotton, livestock, fruits, vegetables, and seafood from small producers to resell in large quantities to central markets or food processing companies. Public warehouses store bulk shipments and break them up for resale in smaller quantities. Resident buying offices offer a collection of merchandise such as apparel from various manufacturers for resale to small retailers who cannot afford to go to market frequently.

Trade Show Planning and Management

Industry trade associations or trade-show management organizations sponsor trade shows that enable producers, wholesalers, retailers, and customers to view and discuss their industry's product offerings. These shows vary in size and function and take months, sometime years, to organize. Because of their increasing popularity over the past ten years, trade show planning and management offer many new marketing career opportunities. In addition to the exposition or show manager, marketing professionals from marketing research, advertising, sales promotion, and public relations work together to make the trade show a success.

Show managers have a variety of responsibilities. First, they must arrange lodging, meals, and transportation for show exhibitors. Second, they must arrange for preparation of exhibit directories, organize display space and equipment, and hire temporary personnel such as receptionists and clerks to work before and during the show. Third, they must direct the marketing effort to attract exhibitors and attendees to the show and provide them with information. In addition to job opportunities with industry trade associations and trade-show management companies, exhibitors hire marketing specialists to determine shows in which to participate, to plan the exhibit, and to staff it with sales personnel. Exhibitors may also hire exhibit designers, who specialize in creating the most positive impact for a company and its products, and contractors who build the booth.

THE GROWTH OF DIRECT MARKETING

The tremendous growth in direct marketing or nonstore selling is another testimony to the desire of the American public to shop quickly and easily. From the company standpoint, direct marketing lowers selling costs because selling via mail, telephone, or computer is less expensive than in-person sales calls. In 1993 Americans spent roughly $60 billion through direct-marketing media such as catalogs and TV shopping channels. That's about 2.8 percent of the retail market and this figure is expected to rise to 15 percent over the next decade.

Mail-order shopping is nothing new to small-town residents. Mail-order houses such as Sears and Montgomery Ward began with the expansion of railroads and the postal service after the Civil War, offering rural shoppers convenience and low prices. The mail-order business has continued to grow—in recent years at about 15 percent per year. Today, a variety of methods are effectively used to reach shoppers in towns and cities of all sizes: direct selling, direct response retailing, database marketing, direct mail, and telemarketing. The growth in direct marketing has created many career opportunities for professionals both in sales and other areas of promotion such as advertising and sales promotion.

Direct marketing is conducted by firms who sell products of other companies and firms and individuals who sell their own products. Every imaginable type of product is sold through direct marketing—apparel, plants, computers, portraits, aluminum siding, pay-per-view television, even steamy romance novels personalized with customers' names used for the major characters.

DIRECT SELLING

Direct (door-to-door) selling, also called direct retailing, is almost an American tradition. Many of us have sets of encyclopedias, the *Great Books of the Western World*, and vacuum cleaners to prove it. For years we have watched Dagwood Bumstead wage war on door-to-door peddlers who are both resourceful and determined. Direct selling is defined as the marketing of products directly to customers through personal explanation and demonstration in their homes or businesses. Direct sales representatives receive training in ingenious ways to sell a product, including demonstrations. Although direct selling comprises only 1 percent of retail sales, it nonetheless contributes roughly $9 billion annually to the U. S. economy. Nearly four million independent salespersons are employed in full- or part-time positions. Avon, the largest cosmetics firm in the world, employs nearly one million door-to-door representatives. They work autonomously, setting their own time tables. Other well-known direct sales companies include Amway Corporation, Kirby Company, Mary Kay Cosmetics, Inc., and World Book.

Although actual door-to-door selling is decreasing as more and more women begin to work outside the home, party-plan selling, institutionalized by Tupperware, is still going strong. Party-plan salespersons recruit hosts or hostesses to give parties at which they demonstrate and sell their products.

Requirements for direct selling careers include a pleasant, outgoing personality and a lot of initiative. A high school education with some courses in speech and business is helpful. Although a college education is not required, courses in business, marketing, psychology, advertising, and sales promotion would be beneficial.

DIRECT RESPONSE RETAILING

Marketers advertise their products in magazines, in newspapers, on radio, and on television. In direct response retailing, also called direct response advertising, an address or phone number is given so consumers can write or call to place an order. Credit cards and toll-free numbers have enhanced this type of marketing. Often marketers hire service bureaus to handle calls and take orders.

Approximately ten years ago, the home-shopping industry was born. Home Shopping Network and QVC Network dominate the nationwide market, selling such items as jewelry, housewares, consumer electronics, apparel, and toys to millions of viewers. Computerized voice-response call-handling systems process calls efficiently and cost-effectively. Sales continue to grow, and the home-shopping networks have also begun to use such marketing tools as celebrity endorsements and direct mail coupons.The concept of target marketing is having an impact on home-shopping networks. For example, Home Shopping Network and Black Entertainment Network are testing a cable shopping program geared to black viewers that will reach over thirty-four million households.

DATABASE MARKETING

Database marketing is revolutionizing the way we perceive selling today. Sometimes called relationship marketing or one-on-one marketing, it involves the collection of volumes of information on groups or individuals. Information collected from coupons, warranty cards, sweepstakes, or given at the time of purchase is combined with publicly recorded information such as real estate records. Through sophisticated statistical techniques and high-powered computer technology, this information is refined to identify specific consumer groups who share characteristics such as income, brand loyalties, and buying practices. These groups or individuals are then targeted as possible markets for new products, recipients of coupons, and entries to lists of potential customers which may be used, sold, or rented. The American Student List Company of Great Neck, New York, sells lists of students, their schools, and their home addresses from kindergarten through graduate school at a rate of fifty dollars per thousand names. Such lists are sometimes offered for rent to companies. Based on demographic data such as income, number of people in the household, geographical location, homeowners, or college major, lists can be tailored for specific company needs. Sources such as birth and wedding announcements, magazine and catalog subscription lists, and professional membership directories are used to create mailing lists. One way to ensure being on numerous lists is to make a purchase through the mail or to be on a catalog subscription list. For example, consumers who purchase plants through the mail from one company are very likely to receive a catalog or brochure through the mail from another company offering plants. The same is true for clothing or any other product.

TELEMARKETING

Marketing done over the telephone is called telemarketing. Since the mid-1970s, the number of businesses that employ telemarketers has increased dramatically. Some firms have in-house telemarketing departments, but most use the services of telemarketing agencies organized much like advertising agencies and direct mail firms. Telemarketing is sometimes used with direct mail or other advertising techniques. Inbound telemarketing involves receiving calls from prospective customers as a result of direct response retailing. These calls may be to place orders, seek information, or make complaints. In outbound telemarketing, the marketer contacts prospective customers by phone to solicit sales. Telemarketers work from prepared scripts written to keep the consumer interested while encouraging purchase of the product or attempting to arrange a sales presentation. Telemarketing may be done from an office or a home phone, making it a convenient job for the physically handicapped or for parents of small children. Aluminum siding companies, photographic studios, and companies offering warranties on products recently purchased use outbound telemarketing regularly. Some firms use computerized phone systems that automatically dial a phone number and play a recorded message.

Telemarketing has experienced explosive growth in recent years. The roughly $100 billion-a-year industry has a growth rate of 30 percent per year. With this growth has come an opportunity for con artists to take advantage of an unwitting public. Telemarketing scams have increased in number and scammers have been able to move their illegal activities from state to state in the absence of federal legislation. Both houses of Congress are now reviewing a proposed law that would provide for the banning of telemarketing scammers nationwide. Passage of this law would alleviate the problem.

Telemarketing professionals are in demand. Telemarketing directors manage direct marketing operations, negotiate telephone contracts, and incorporate new telecommunications technologies into the marketing effort. Telesales representatives report to the director. Normally telemarketers are trained on the job. A pleasant telephone voice and the ability to handle rejection graciously are required since most calls do not result in sales. Some college is helpful for advancement to supervisor positions. The growing need for middle managers who function as training managers or operations managers will guarantee opportunities for advancement. These managers hire, train, and motivate new personnel; prepare reports; make projections; and coordinate operations. Promotion to telemarketing manager usually requires several years of experience and a college degree in business, marketing, or a related area.

Full-time telemarketers can earn $300 a week or more. Hourly rates vary from $4 to $10 an hour. Workers may earn straight salary, commission only, or a combination of the two.

CATALOG RETAILING

Spiegel, L.L. Bean, Eddie Bauer, and J.C. Penney are among thousands of companies that offer merchandise for sale through catalogs. Growth in catalog sales peaked in the late 1970s and early 1980s. Although growth has slowed , the catalog business is growing at a faster rate than in-store retailing. Looking for a new way to spur sales, Spiegel introduced videologs, which are videotape catalogs. These videologs quickly produced orders at roughly twice the rate of the paper catalogs. Electronic catalogs will be more important in the future.

Catalog sales enable shoppers to select items from a vast array. Most catalog companies have liberal return policies. More and more products will be offered in new and innovative ways through catalog retailing. Though catalog retailing primarily employs order takers, there are key positions for buyers, advertising professionals, and marketing managers. New technology now enables consumers to place orders electronically.

DIRECT MAIL

Direct mail is one of the fastest growing segments of the direct marketing industry. It includes catalogs sent through the mail, promotional letters, and other materials offering products for sale. Direct mail is used to produce leads, inquiries, orders, or increase store traffic. Another benefit of direct mail is that it enables producers to determine exactly who is buying their products. Thus advertising campaigns can target identified markets. Specialized direct mail firms and advertising agencies offer direct mail services. In both cases, account, research, creative, and media departments work together to develop the direct mail campaign. The campaign focuses on established and potential customers. Companies may purchase targeted mailing lists from list brokers. List management firms compile, sort, update, and rent lists of names. They employ list managers; sales personnel; computer personnel for data entry, programming, and analysis; and research personnel.

DEMAND FOR SALES REPRESENTATIVES

The Bureau of Labor statistics projects large numbers of new jobs in manufacturing and wholesale trade sales and in marketing and sales worker supervisors. The growth and success of direct mail is due in large part to being able to target market segments through the use of database marketing. That these databases are an invasion of privacy and cause a veritable paper blizzard of advertisements for those who order by mail cannot be denied. Similarly, unsolicited phone calls, even to unlisted telephone numbers selected at random, from telemarketers are becoming a nuisance. These issues will bear closer scrutiny as the growth in nonstore marketing continues.

It is likely that, considering the demographics of the American public and the trends in lifestyles, direct marketing will continue to grow at a faster rate than in-store marketing. Although fraudulent offers and questionable product claims cause consumers to be somewhat wary, products offered at reduced prices that can be ordered simply by dialing a toll-free number are very attractive.

WHAT SALES REPRESENTATIVES EARN

Sales representatives' earnings are very difficult to project. Sales representatives may be paid on straight commission, thus income is a percent of sales made. It can fluctuate greatly depending on peak and trough selling periods within the industry, the economy, and the ability of the sales person. Sometimes sales personnel are paid a set salary plus a commission on sales. Some are paid a straight salary. Employers normally pay at least some commission as an incentive for sales representatives to generate more sales and thereby benefit directly from their efforts.

Numerous types of bonuses are given by employers. The most common bonuses are given for meeting sales quotas. Project launch bonuses are common in pharmaceutical and high-tech sales if a large percentage of the targeted accounts sign on. Bonuses are given for account penetration where sales are increased in specified accounts or product lines. Manufacturers offer sales personnel bonuses for increasing intermediary participation in product training or gaining information about competitor business. Calling on personnel outside of purchasing who might influence a distributor's buying decision might be awarded with a bonus. Many companies use bonuses as incentives. Insurance and real estate companies tend to favor contests and prizes such as trips.

Sales representatives must sell in order to earn their commissions. Employers normally offer beginners salary plus commission until they reach a predetermined sales level. Another common practice is to let beginners draw income against future commissions. If they are unable to generate sales, sales representatives quit or get fired. Those who cannot sell cannot support themselves in a sales profession.

In areas such as real estate, insurance, and financial services sales, a broker's annual income can be very large. However, in these areas only the top 10 percent normally make a lot of money. If an individual has the ability to be in this top percent group, there is no limit to income; it usually rivals or exceeds that of top management.

Figure 6.2 gives a rough idea of what manufacturing and wholesale sales representatives earn.

Figure 6.2 Salaries of Manufacturing and Wholesale Sales Representatives

Level of experience		Type of product	
	Consumer goods	Industrial goods	Services
Trainee	$25,000	$30,500	$24,000
Middle level	40,000	42,500	37,000
Top level	68,000	59,500	61,500

Salaries in telemarketing are highest in the West, where in-house telesales representatives earn base plus bonus or commission of approximately $31,000. The average nationwide is about $25,000 and the range is from $12,000 to $36,000. Telemarketing managers or directors average $80,000 in the West, and $63,000 nationally.

SOURCES OF INFORMATION

Information on wholesaling and industrial sales can be obtained from the following professional associations:

Association of Industry Manufacturers Representatives
222 Merchandise Mart Plaza, Suite 1360
Chicago, IL 60654
(312)464-0092

Manufacturers' Agents National Association
23016 Mill Creek Road
P.O. Box 3467
Laguna Hills, CA 92654
(714)859-4040

The Employers Group
1150 South Olive Street, Suite 2300
P.O. Box 15013
Los Angeles, CA 90015
(213)748-0421

National Association of Wholesaler-Distributors
1725 K Street, N.W.
Washington, DC 20006
(202)872-0885

National Council of Salesmen's Organizations
358 Fifth Avenue, Room 1010
New York, NY 10016
(718)835-4591

National Association of Business and Industrial Saleswomen
90 Corona, Suite 1407
Denver, CO 80218
(303)777-7257

National Association of Catalog Showroom Merchandisers
P.O. Box 736
East Northport, NY 11731
(516)754-6041

International Association of Sales Professionals
13 East 37th Street, Eighth Floor
New York, NY 10016-2821
(212)683-9755

Sales and Marketing Executives International
Statler Office Tower, 458
Cleveland, OH 44115
(216)771-6650

Students may obtain career and scholarship information
from the following sales fraternity associated with SMEI:
Pi Sigma Epsilon
155 East Capitol Drive, Suite 9
Hartland, WI 53029
(414)367-5600

For information on trade show planning, write:

Trade Show Bureau
1660 Lincoln Street, Suite 2080
Denver, CO 80264
(303)860-7626

Those interested in direct marketing can write:

American Telemarketing Association
444 North Larchmont Boulevard, Suite 200
Los Angeles, CA 90004
(213)463-2330

Direct Marketing Association
11 West 42nd Street
New York, NY 10036-8096
(212)768-7277

Direct Selling Association
1776 K Street N.W., Suite 600
Washington, DC 20006
(202)293-5760

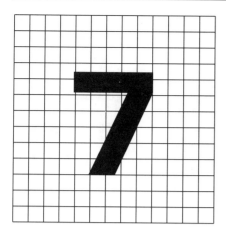

CAREERS IN RETAILING

Total annual U.S. retail sales exceed $2 trillion. Over 4.75 million people hold jobs in retail sales, 20 percent of all private sector jobs. Roughly one out of every seven full-time workers is employed in retailing. Thousands more hold part-time jobs in retailing. And thousands open their own retail businesses each year. Therefore, retailing has a vital role in driving the U.S. economy.

Retailing is a combination of activities involved in selling goods and services directly to consumers for personal or household use. The activities of retail establishments include buying items from manufacturers and wholesalers, advertising, accounting, data processing, materials management, and personal selling, the latter being the key to successful retailing. Retail establishments come in all sizes from Sears, the largest with sales in excess of $30 billion, to the tiny shop on the corner with one employee—the owner. Figure 7.1 shows types of retail stores.

This chapter focuses on in-store retailing. (Chapter 6 discussed nonstore retailing.) Retail professions fall into two groups: those involved in purchasing the goods offered for sale in retail stores, including merchandise managers, buyers, and assistant buyers; and those involved in selling goods to the public, including department managers and salespeople. This chapter explores these and other retail professions.

TRENDS IN RETAILING

The 1980s were profitable years for retailers. According to a *Business Week* article of November 26, 1990, the U.S. has eighteen feet of retail space for every man, woman, and child—twice the amount in 1972. Today many shopping centers and new stores are deserted or advertise going-out-of-business

Figure 7.1 Types of Retail Stores

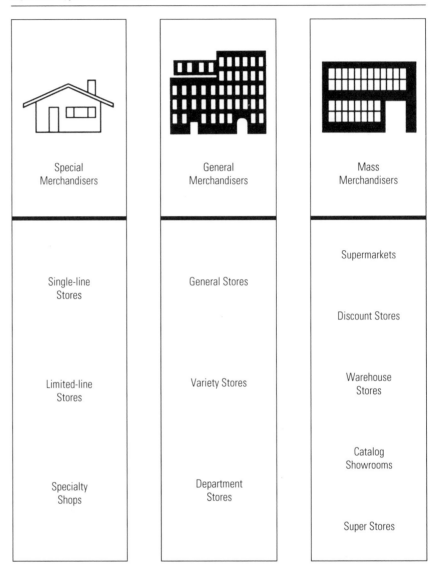

sales. The most successful retailers such as Dillards, The Gap, Wal-Mart Stores, and The Limited will dominate the field, but will have to work hard to grow during the leaner 1990s.

Retailers are staking out new territory in Canada. Wal-Mart acquired 122 Woolco stores and is converting them into Wal-Marts; Home Depot entered Canada by buying 75 percent of Canada's Aikenhead's Home Improvement Warehouse chain; Staples acquired the Business Depot chain; in the past three years, The Gap doubled the number of Canada stores; and Price/Costco will open ten more warehouse stores this year alone. Wal-Mart, the United States' number one retailer, is also expanding rapidly in Mexico. Industry experts note that the challenge to retailers will be to avoid high levels of debt, target specific markets, and use technology to reduce cost and improve service.

Along with discount stores, warehouse clubs, and outlet malls, price-conscious consumers are looking for bargains in used merchandise. Recycling as a retail trend is evident in the growth of used-merchandise stores such as Grow Biz International, Play It Again Sports, Once Upon a Child, and American Rag. Vintage clothing, once considered camp, is now considered chic. These stores do not have a Goodwill or pawn shop atmosphere, but feel and operate like any other retail establishment.

Specialty Stores

Another of the major trends in retailing of the 1980s was the rise in popularity of the specialty store. Specialty store sales grew roughly 60 percent faster than department store sales. This change in shopping habits of the American public has been attributed to the needs of the increasing number of working women. Such specialty stores as apparel stores, bookstores, toy stores, sporting goods stores, and others offer a narrow product line but a deep range within the line. They stock more styles, colors, sizes, or models with a variety of features, giving the shopper more choices. Shopping is less complicated and time-consuming because there are no long lines or confusing departments. Specialty stores are handy for lunch-hour shopping or quick stops after work. If a specific item is unavailable, shop owners are usually willing to order it and call customers when it arrives. More businesses keep popping up to fill the new strip shopping centers—more convenient than large shopping malls. These new businesses will be discussed in chapter 10 in the section on entrepreneurship.

Variety Stores

General merchandise department and variety stores have undergone some dramatic changes over the past decade. Bloomingdale's, Macy's, Saks Fifth Avenue, Marshall Field's, and other department stores around the country are synonymous with style. Although these stores have numerous departments, including toys, furniture, sporting goods, books, and housewares, their real strength is clothing. In order to compete with discount and specialty stores, department stores have added both budget shops and designer departments.. For those in fashion-related merchandising and sales, the greater emphasis on clothing is good news. The 1950s through the 1970s saw the development of suburban shopping centers and the deterioration of downtown shopping. However, throughout the 1980s downtown shopping malls began to develop. These malls contain fashionable department stores, specialty shops, and restaurants that cater to tourists, conventioneers, and lunch-hour shoppers in the downtown area.

Woolworth's is changing from a variety to a specialty merchant. Closing many of its variety stores (former five-and-dimes), Woolworth's opened eleven hundred new stores in 1988, including Champs, Kids Mart, Herald Square, and Lady Foot Locker. Walgreen Company, on the other hand, has started to sell beer, wine, soda, snacks, milk, bread, and frozen TV dinners along with the usual drugstore type of merchandise. Though prescription and nonprescription drugs are the fastest growing portion of Walgreen's business and likely to remain so as the population ages, the convenience-store approach has worked well.

Discount Stores

Mass merchandising retailers offer wide variety at discount prices in large self-service stores. Opportunities in sales are greatly reduced, purchasing is centralized, and services are nearly nonexistent. However, management opportunities exist in these stores, and many chains are experiencing phenomenal growth. Discount stores, super stores, warehouse clubs, and warehouse and catalog showrooms are examples of mass merchandising retailers.

In 1990 there were 183 factory outlet malls in the nation. That number had grown to 294 in August 1994, with more in the planning stage. Outlet malls generate more sales per square foot than the large regional malls. Initially these outlet malls contained only manufacturers' shops; some contain only upscale manufacturers. Now, however, some malls are renting space to discount houses as well. The trend toward factory outlet shops and discount malls is likely to continue. Some conjecture suggests that the market will soon be saturated and that some failures are inevitable.

Wal-Mart, needing new avenues of growth, acquired Wholesale Club and Pace to increase its share of the warehouse club business. Sam's and Price/Costco now share 90 percent of the warehouse club market. Specialty retailers such as Home Depot, Office Depot, The Sports Authority, and PetSmart have imitated the format of the large variety wholesale clubs. A widening gap between rich and poor is attributed to numerous factors, including declines in the manufacturing segment of the economy, a lessening union influence to keep salaries up, and stiffer educational requirements for better-paying jobs. Some retailers have begun to cater more to low-income shoppers. The future looks promising for discount stores and warehouse clubs.

Technology

Interactive networks will have an effect on retailing. This change won't occur overnight because of the expense of the new technology and natural skepticism of things radically different. Initially interactive shopping will probably gain popularity in niches such as recorded music and software, but anything offered through TV shopping networks or catalogs can be sold interactively. Consumer acceptance will be the key to the success of the new technologies.

Retailing today is placing greater emphasis on technology and professional management. Supermarkets and large discount stores have used computerized cash registers and point-of-sale terminals for years. As these tools gain in popularity, up-to-the-minute sales information will be available to more and more retailers. Executives with both merchandising and management skills who can increase profits and worker productivity through use of the new technology will be in demand. Large discount retailers exact careful control over their inventory by tying into their suppliers electronically. Electronic intercompany inventory management enables retailers and their suppliers to maintain inventory as needed and will change the way buyers work.

RETAIL SALES

Retailing professionals are primarily employed in sales. Successful retail sales people know their merchandise and are very effective in meeting the public. Customers come into retail establishments to purchase specific items, comparison shop, or merely to browse. The people who deal directly with these customers can make or break a business. An ability to communicate well, a courteous manner, and a positive attitude are three prerequisites for success in selling any product. Many people reject the idea of a career in sales because they dislike the hard sell. It also repels customers. The successful salesperson finds out what customers want and need, determines what merchandise meets this need, persuades the customer to buy it, and makes the customer feel good about the purchase. Essentially, the best selling is actually helping the customer buy. Customer service is the real key to successful selling.

Mass Merchandising

The most basic type of sales and customer service occurs in mass merchandising, where customer inquiries usually have to do with whether the store stocks an item and where it can be found. Knowledge of store layout and merchandise is necessary. Although these positions do not involve commissions and do involve stocking shelves more than actual selling, they are good jobs for those with little formal education and for students, providing both full-time and part-time opportunities. They offer experience that other employers often seek and can lead to supervisory positions in sales.

Specialty Sales

Sales work in fashion apparel, cosmetics, and numerous other product lines requires greater product knowledge and sometimes requires special skills. For example, cosmetics salespeople sometimes give demonstrations as part of their sales presentation. Whether employed in a department of a large store or a small specialty shop, good salespeople must demonstrate friendly interest in their customers, a willingness to help, and considerable diplomacy.

Some clothes do not look good on some figures. Rather than selling a customer something that isn't flattering (a realization that the customer will reach sooner or later), a good salesperson will tactfully show the customer something that looks better. Helping customers involves much more than ringing up sales.

Commission Sales

In selling such big-ticket items as cars, computers, and appliances, salespeople must not only know the capabilities of their own products, they must also know why their products are superior to those of their competitors. Therefore, they need to be familiar with competing products. Salespeople working on commission can have a large income if they generate many sales.

The Retail Sales Professional

To be effective, a sales professional should

1. Ascertain the wants and needs of customers.
2. Be familiar with the market and competition.
3. Understand and describe product features and uses.
4. Be able to explain the benefits to customers.
5. Learn effective selling techniques.
6. Know the importance of customer service.
7. Develop a positive attitude toward work.

Although in retail sales customers come to the store, a salesperson needs both initiative and a customer-service orientation to close more sales. Too often in large department stores the customer must seek out the salesperson. The salesperson with the initiative to approach the customer is far more likely to make the sale.

In retailing, it is important to understand the customer. For example, Brooks Brothers has catered to generations of men desiring traditional men's tailoring. When Marks & Spencer acquired Brooks Brothers, they shocked many loyal customers by installing escalators in 1989 and putting shirts and sweaters on open tables rather than in glass cases. These "innovations" along with jazzy new ads to attract a younger clientele brought a host of complaints from regular customers. Every successful retail establishment has a solid customer base. Understanding the likes and dislikes of the store's customers and keeping them happy while luring new customers is important to sales personnel and management.

Whether selling goods or services, the selling professional must be reliable and responsive. The customer may not always be easy to deal with. Selling requires self-control and diplomacy. Everyone does not have the temperament for selling to the public, but for those who do, sales can be a lucrative and rewarding profession. Although sales positions offer the greatest number of job opportunities within retailing, there are other career options for individuals from a variety of educational backgrounds.

SALES MANAGEMENT

Sales management trainees may be recruited from the sales staff or from the pool of recent college graduates. MBAs have no real advantage in landing beginning retail management positions, though if hired they may earn slightly higher salaries. In retailing, hands-on experience is the real key. Compared to other marketing careers, experience is fairly easy to obtain by working in a part-time retail sales position while in college. Though often minimum-wage jobs, these part-time positions provide the necessary experience to obtain a good job after graduation. Large department stores actively recruit on college campuses, which provides an excellent way for prospective graduates to make an initial contact. Applicants should ask about the company's management training program. Most large companies offer them.

Beginning as a department manager trainee, novices work with experienced managers throughout the store to observe all aspects of store operations. Under supervision, trainees handle staff scheduling, customer complaints, and record keeping. Once a trainee has demonstrated the ability to effectively supervise staff, work well with customers, and make good quick decisions balancing the welfare of the store and the customer, the individual is promoted to manager of a small department.

The next level of promotion is usually to a larger department where the manager supervises more staff, handles more merchandise, and manages a larger budget in accordance with store policies. Such duties as scheduling workers, handling customer service requests and complaints, and monitoring how well merchandise is selling are all part of the job. Sales staff development is also important because, when promoted, effective department managers have already trained their replacements. Retail sales managers are usually given broad goals containing sales and profit expectations. How to reach or exceed these goals is up to the manager. If the department is exceptionally profitable as a result of the manager's skill, promotion to group sales manager is likely. Directing several department managers and coordinating a sizable portion of store operations effectively may qualify an individual for assistant store manager, then store manager. The best retail store managers are selected for top corporate positions. Upwardly mobile managers are often targeted early in their careers and may be required to relocate every few years.

MERCHANDISE BUYING AND MANAGEMENT

Buyers purchase the merchandise that the store will sell. They decide what products will be offered for sale, arrange purchases from manufacturers, and set retail prices. Decisions depend on knowledge of customer tastes, changing trends, and a balance of quality and affordability. To make these decisions, buyers study marketing research reports, industry and trade publications, and the direction of the economy. Because of the responsibility involved in spending large amounts of the store's money, the training period for buyers can range from two to five years. The entry-level merchandising position for college graduates is assistant buyer. After some store training, usually in sales, an assistant buyer works under a merchandising supervisor. Duties usually include speaking with manufacturers and placing approved orders for merchandise, inspecting new merchandise, and supervising its distribution throughout the department. During the first two to five years in buying, the novice becomes acquainted with manufacturers' lines, the store's needs, and the competition and begins to recommend products for purchase. Once promoted to buyer, duties expand to analyzing customer needs and choosing products to meet them. The role of the buyer is critical to the success of any retail establishment. For example, The Gap has decreased its in-store basics, denim and T-shirts, to add a few new items such as flowing skirts, embroidered tops, hats, shoes, and workout clothes. Cutting down on the number of basic items puts more pressure on the buyer to choose the right merchandise mix. Buyers normally begin in small departments and are promoted to larger departments.

The most promising buyers become merchandise managers whose primary duties are to supervise buyers. They oversee the department's budget , deciding how money should be divided among the buyers. Merchandise managers have a great impact on their store's image, its product offerings, and the direction of styles. They must develop a mix of brands to generate the most sales and profits, taking care to keep store brands from overwhelming other brands. Distribution managers oversee the movement of merchandise. They are responsible for receipt, ticketing, storage, and distribution of a store's inventory. The growing problem of customer and employee theft has resulted in a new management position—loss-prevention manager, whose duties include tracking inventory, price overrides, refunds, and employee purchases. Point-of-sale and electronic article surveillance systems are also used for security in theft-plagued retail outlets. Buyers who have been promoted through various management levels often reach the position of corporate merchandise manager. In this position, they may approve buying decisions for several stores in one state or in an entire region.

The bread and butter of large department stores is apparel. To fill the specialized position of fashion coordinator an individual needs a background in fashion design, a portfolio to show artistic talent, a keen sense of style, good taste, and an awareness of sound business practices. Some large department stores employ fashion coordinators to work with buyers in selecting merchandise. Although glamorous work in that it may involve overseas buying, the position of fashion coordinator is not a step up the corporate ladder. It does afford those with backgrounds in art or fashion merchandising an exciting and satisfying outlet for their artistic talents.

Another position requiring an art background is display designer. Large retailers design window and interior displays to promote sales. Recent graduates begin as apprentices and are trained on the job. Competition is very stiff for positions in fashion coordination and display as opportunities are very limited.

OPPORTUNITIES IN RETAILING

Retailing will continue to employ huge numbers of sales representatives. It is estimated that approximately 862,000 new jobs for sales representatives and supervisors will be created each year until the year 2005. Demand and salaries can vary considerably, depending on the industry. Full-time retail sales people earn from $17,000 to $50,000 or more. Retail sales manager trainees, beginners with degrees in merchandising, marketing, or some area of business earn from $28,000 to $41,000. Experienced managers earn from $46,000 to 78,000. Sales managers of the largest stores can earn over $100,000 with bonuses.

SOURCES OF INFORMATION

Staying up-to-date on trends is essential to retail professionals, especially buyers and merchandise and department managers. Such periodicals as *Advertising Age*, *Chain Store Age Executive*, *Discount Store News*, *The Fashion Newsletter*, *Inside Retailing Newsletter*, *Journal of Retailing*, *Stores*, and *Women's Wear Daily* are available in most public and college libraries. Directories of retailers can be found in the reference section of the library, including *Fairchild's Financial Manual of Retail Stores*, *Nationwide Directory—Mass Market Merchandisers*, and *Sheldon's Retail Directory of the U.S. and Canada*.

As in other fields, retailing associations are another excellent source of inside information. Some are listed below.

American Marketing Association
250 South Wacker Drive, Suite 200
Chicago, IL 60606
(312)648-0536

National Retail Federation
701 Pennsylvania Avenue, N.W., Suite 710
Washington, DC 20004
(202)783-7971

General Merchandise Distributors Council
1275 Lake Plaza Drive
Colorado Springs, CO 80906
(719)576-4260

International Mass Retail Association
1901 Pennsylvania Avenue, N.W., Tenth Floor
Washington, DC 20006
(202)861-0774

National Association for Professional Saleswomen
1730 North Lynn Street, Suite 502
Arlington, VA 22209
(800)823-6277

National Association of Retail Dealers of America
10 22nd Street
Lombard, IL 60148
(708)953-8950

National Association of Service Merchandising
118 South Clinton Street, Suite 300
Chicago, IL 60661-3628
(312)876-9494

International Association of Sales Professionals
13 E. 37th Street, Eighth Floor
New York, NY 10016-2821
(212)683-9755

Sales and Marketing Executives International
Statler Office Tower, No. 458
Cleveland, OH 44115
(216)771-6650

Women in Sales Association
Eight Madison Avenue
P.O. Box M
Valhalla, NY 10595
(914)946-3802

Many industries have their own associations:

Cosmetics, Toiletry and Fragrance Association
1101 17th Street, N.W., Suite 300
Washington, DC 20036
(202)331-1770

Electronic Industries Association
2001 Pennsylvania, N.W.
Washington, DC 20006-1813
(202)457-4900

The Fashion Association
475 Park Avenue, S., Seventeenth Floor
New York, NY 10016
(212)683-5665

Apparel Retailers of America
2011 I Street, N.W., Suite 250
Washington, DC 20006
(202)347-1932

National Sporting Goods Association
Lake Center Plaza Building
1699 Wall Street
Mount Prospect, IL 60056-5780
(708)439-4000

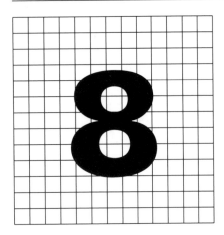

CAREERS IN CORPORATE MARKETING MANAGEMENT

No matter how high in the company individuals rise, they never stop selling. This story appeared in the May 2, 1994, issue of Fortune magazine. Billionaire investor Warren Buffett accepted an invitation in early 1993 to speak to the directors and top executives of General Motors. Jack Smith, GM's CEO, found out that Buffett didn't drive a GM car. Buffett explained that he switched from Cadillacs to a Lincoln Town Car because it had dual airbags. In February 1994 Buffett received a note from Smith informing him that Cadillac was now equipped with airbags that not only handled the driver and the passenger in the end seat but also the passenger sitting in the middle. Buffet was so impressed with Smith's memory and dogged salesmanship that he promised to buy a Cadillac the next time he purchased a car.

Throughout the functional areas of corporate marketing—marketing research, product development, advertising, sales promotion, public relations, and sales—outstanding individuals advance to management levels. The top position is vice-president of marketing, who has authority over all marketing activities in a corporation. Often a marketing vice-president advances to the position of chief executive officer (CEO). Figure 8.1 is a corporate organizational chart showing chain of command and levels of authority. This hierarchy varies from firm to firm depending on the number of management levels and how marketing functions are organized within the firm.

Corporations have streamlined management considerably over the past decade. In the 1970s it was customary to have as many as twelve to fifteen levels of supervision in large corporations. Today five or six levels is the norm. This is the result of major restructuring brought about by a wave of acquisitions and divestitures, increased global competition, an attempt at creating a more entrepreneurial environment to foster new product development,

Figure 8.1 Top and Middle Levels of Corporate Marketing Management

Chief Executive Officer Vice-President Marketing National Sales Manager	Top Management
Regional Sales Managers Products and Category Managers Department Managers	1st Tier Middle Management
District Sales Manager Brand and Product Managers	2nd Tier Middle Management

and a recessionary economy. The reduction of middle-level managers has increased both the complexity and the pressures of management positions.

THE RESTRUCTURING OF CORPORATE MANAGEMENT

The 1980s were characterized by thousands of mergers, acquisitions, and divestitures. As companies and pieces of companies were bought and sold, hundreds of thousands of managers and professionals were forced to change jobs or retire early. In many cases, middle-level management positions were never refilled. Major reorganizations took place in companies. Top management realized that if the firm was to compete in a more competitive, rapidly changing business environment, it had to respond more rapidly to change. Though reducing costs in increasingly tight economic conditions was a factor in not replacing many middle-level managers, an even more important factor was the ability of a leaner corporation to introduce products into the market more efficiently.

For years, small companies have received the most credit for introducing new technology into the marketplace. One of the reasons for this is the efficiency of a less formal corporate structure. While new products ideas were being reviewed by fifteen levels of management in large companies, small companies, functioning as entrepreneurial teams, had already moved a product from the drawing board to the marketplace. The message was clear—until large corporations became more entrepreneurial in both philosophy and practice, they would be unable to beat their small competitors into the marketplace with new products.

Big companies responded to the challenge by creating more project or product development teams. These teams were given the authority to operate fairly autonomously both in fulfilling goals and competing for company resources, as was described in chapter 3 on product development. Product managers reported directly to top marketing managers. Because the teams were entrepreneurial in spirit yet part of a large corporation, the term *intrepreneuring* was coined.

With fewer levels of management and tighter budgets, companies are unable to reward managers with promotions and raises as they once did. However, fewer job titles and pay grades make it easier to base raises on performance rather than seniority. One way companies motivate promising young managers is with a lateral or sideways move that offers a new challenge and enables young managers to learn another part of company operations. Giving more responsibility and autonomy to subordinates is another way to keep young managers from getting bored. Overseas assignments for managers are inevitable as companies expand their global operations. At companies where a large percentage of sales are foreign, an overseas assignment is necessary for promotion to top management. Finally, more companies are offering up-and-coming executives midcareer breaks by sending them to management development programs designed by business schools especially for executives.

MARKETING MANAGERS

Top-level executives determine an organization's mission and make policy. The executive vice-president for marketing directs overall marketing policy, the effect of which is felt at every level and function of the marketing process. The marketing management concept permeating the field today, as described in chapter 1, is broader in scope because of the increasingly complex business and economic environment in which the firms of today must operate. Top-level production and finance managers must be convinced that marketing policies will enable the firm to meet its overall goals and objectives. Considerable time is spent by the top marketing executive in selling these policies to the CEO and other top officers.

All marketing managers are involved in planning, implementing, and controlling marketing activities and decisions. These functions are common to all managers, but marketing managers at the top of the organization are primarily involved in planning. Planning includes setting objectives and standards of performance and developing strategies and tactics to implement those objectives. Marketing strategy addresses such issues as what markets to enter, what products to offer, how to allocate marketing resources, and, for large corporations, what companies to buy. Marketing executives must make such global decisions in consultation with finance, production, and sales executives. Objectives and strategies are communicated to lower level marketing managers who then develop the detailed marketing strategy required to implement the plans.

MIDDLE MANAGERS AND SUPERVISORS

Implementation involves organizing, staffing, directing, and coordinating the organization's resources. All marketing managers are involved in implementation activities to some extent. But unlike top managers, who spend most of their time in strategic planning, middle-level managers such as department heads and project team leaders are primarily involved in implementation. Hiring staff, assigning duties, directing and overseeing projects, distributing the budget throughout the department, and such activities are the responsibility of department heads.

Middle-level managers and supervisors whom managers appoint to assist in these activities are responsible for measuring staff performance to see that objectives are met and taking corrective action if they are not. Specific objectives related to deadlines for projects, planned budgets, and sales quotas are measurable. If objectives are not met, it is up to managers to determine whether they were unrealistic, or whether either external unpredictable factors or worker performance is responsible. Corrective action may involve revising objectives, making adjustments to allow for external factors, or working with staff to solve problems.

The work of middle managers and supervisors has been discussed throughout the chapters of this book. They manage staffs of professionals and technicians working in the various activities of marketing. Managers of marketing research, product development, advertising, sales promotion, public relations, and regional sales all report to top-level marketing managers. In the absence of many levels of middle managers, these managers operate their departments more autonomously and have more authority over both activities and budgets. Their offices are usually located close to top management, and communications are considerably less formal than in the huge bureaucracies of the past. Though chain of command is still intact in many organizations where managers at every level formally report to a designated individual, communications are considerably more relaxed and pragmatic in most organizations.

Technology has changed corporate communications forever. Each manager has a personal computer usually hooked into a central computer through local area network (LAN) technology. Branch computers are hooked into the central computer through wide area network (WAN) technology. Thus improved communications technology has enabled the free flow of information throughout the organization. Management information systems (MIS) and decision support systems (DSS) provide a systematic way of disseminating information needed for management decisions. A system is a collection of people, machines, programs, and procedures organized to perform a certain task. Marketing information systems provide marketing managers a steady flow of timely, accurate information from a variety of sources both inside and outside the firm that they can then use to make decisions. Computers and communications technology have reduced the need for managers whose main job was organizing and communicating this type of information.

ADVANCEMENT INTO MANAGEMENT

To succeed on the job and advance into management, marketing professionals should choose the right company, find a mentor, and use whatever resources are available. Choosing the right company is a complicated issue. Company offers to new college graduates may be evaluated in terms of salary, benefits, and growth potential. Chapters 11 and 12 address many issues that will help graduates evaluate the job market and company offers that they will receive. But very little of the internal working of the company can be gleaned from company literature or job interviews. Only when working for a company can an individual learn the intricacies of how decisions are made and where the power resides.

Attracting a Mentor

The single most important action that a new employee takes is finding a mentor. A mentor is an older professional in the same field, preferably making steady career progress up the company ladder. Good mentors offer introductions to people higher up and a good many insights into the unspoken rules in the company. Every company has a unique corporate culture and its own way of doing things. Finding a mentor is not easy. Any mentor worth having is extremely busy and not out looking for proteges. The young employee who shows persistence yet flexibility, works hard to obtain recognition, listens to everything going on in the company before taking strong positions or forming alliances, has clearly stated career goals, and displays confidence and pride as well as ability will attract attention before long. Many employees have followed their mentors right up the hierarchy by filling the positions they vacate on the way up.

Women in Management

It is particularly important for women to have mentors because females are greatly underrepresented in middle and top levels of management in larger companies. Women's salaries lag behind those of men for the same positions. A recent *Business Week* Harris Poll reported that 60 percent of women in management in large corporations identified "a male-dominated corporate culture" as an obstacle to success. Some companies, however, make a concerted effort to remove obstacles to women's advancement into corporate management ranks through programs such as awareness training for men. Some companies even set goals for promoting women.

The August 6, 1990, issue of *Business Week* reported results of a study conducted to identify companies with woman-friendly corporate cultures. The factors considered were numbers of women in key executive positions and on the board of directors, specific efforts to help women advance, and sensitivity to the work/family dilemma. The following six companies rated very highly: Avon, CBS, Dayton-Hudson, Gannett, Kelly Services, and U.S. West. Two of these companies, Avon and Kelly Services, are in women-intensive industries. The next group of companies have made substantial progress in advancing women. It includes American Express, Baxter International, Corning, Honeywell, IBM, Johnson & Johnson, Merck, Monsanto, Pitney Bowes, Reader's Digest, Security Pacific Bank, and Square D. These companies are in a wide variety of industries. Women have fared very well in computer companies, entering in substantial numbers when their skills were very much needed at the birth of the industry. But other industries represented in this group are old conservative industries such as banking and electrical manufacturing. The named companies reversed usual practices to become woman-friendly. Honorable mentions are Digital Equipment, DuPont, Hewlett-Packard, Olin, 3M, and Xerox.

Though women have had to work hard to prove themselves, every successful woman changes a few minds. Women's networks in companies often help other women learn the ropes. It is important for young women aspiring to management positions to be aware of how women are faring at the companies making them offers. Questions to ask at interviews should be what percentage of women hold top management posts? Middle management posts? Do company benefits include extended leaves, flex-time, day-care assistance? The best offer for a new graduate may not come from a woman-friendly company but from a company offering excellent training and development opportunities. Trade-offs are always present in job offers. It is important for both men and women to carefully articulate their short- and long-range goals before entering the job market.

RESOURCES FOR SUCCESS IN MANAGEMENT

Three major areas of resources for professional managers are company training and continuing education, professional organizations, and marketing periodicals.

Management Training and Development

Management training and development is an important ingredient in the success formula for marketing professionals. Without good training and development opportunities, individuals can become stagnant early in their careers. The first question that a job applicant should ask is, "What kind of training and development will the company provide me if I accept this position?" To meet training needs, some companies are allowing employees to select the pace of training that takes place both inside and outside the work environment.

This partnership enables ambitious employees to have more control over training opportunities and to advance at their own rate. In addition to the traditional stand-up lecture, company training programs employ technologies such as interactive video, computer-based training, television courses, and numerous others. *The National Directory of Corporate Training Programs* provides information on such training programs and the companies that offer them.

It is estimated that corporations spend nearly $15 billion a year on formal training programs for managers and professionals, much of it conducted in business schools. Major restructuring in corporations has caused the emphasis of executive training to be placed on organizational transformation rather than personal development. Business schools are offering programs designed for specific corporations. These programs as well as in-house programs are geared to meet specific goals or to transform corporate culture. For example, General Electric Company sends managers to learn how to develop markets in the fast-growing economies of Asia. Ford uses management development to encourage closer cooperation across disciplines to create more product-oriented marketing people and vice versa. Cigna Corporation uses team-building activities to tackle real company problems, culminating in recommendations to senior management.

Going to work for a company that offers its employees training and development programs and support should be an important career objective. Continuing education programs offered through colleges and universities enable individuals to increase their chances of promotion. Many companies pay tuition costs for job-related courses, sometimes entire MBA programs. An MBA is helpful, often necessary, to advance through management ranks. Professionals are responsible for their own training and career development regardless of the type of training and continuing education opportunities an employer provides. Training opportunities are also available to members through their professional organizations. By joining professional organizations as a student, one can take advantage of some early training opportunities and gain a competitive edge.

Professional Management Organizations

Participation in professional organizations is very beneficial to marketing professionals and students. The organizations provide an opportunity for communications among members at meetings and conferences. In addition, a tremendous amount of current information is disseminated through advanced training and seminars sponsored by the organizations. Many offer placement services for new college graduates. The price of membership for students is greatly reduced in most cases.

A good source for names and addresses of professional organizations is the *Encyclopedia of Associations* published annually and found in the reference section of the library. Information includes names, addresses, and phone numbers of professional associations; the date they were founded; the number of current members; a description of the membership; and publications, if any. In addition to the organizations related to specific areas of marketing listed in the various chapters, many marketing managers hold memberships in the following associations:

American Management Association
135 West 50th Street
New York, NY 10020-1201
(212)586-8100

American Marketing Association
250 South Wacker Drive, Suite 200
Chicago, IL 60606
(312)648-0536

Sales and Marketing Executives, International
458 Statler Office Tower
Cleveland, OH 44115
(216)771-6650

International Association of Sales Professionals
13 East 37th Street, Eighth Floor
New York, NY 10016-2821
(212)683-9755

Women in Management
30 North Michigan Avenue, Suite 508
Chicago, IL 60602
(312)263-3636

Management Newsletters and Journals

Many professional associations publish newsletters and journals. Marketing periodicals are excellent sources of general information. An impressive list can be found in *Ulrich's International Periodicals Directory* in the reference section of the library. It is published annually by R.R. Bowker Company, New York and London. A good many marketing periodicals can be found in public and university libraries. Most marketing professionals subscribe to a number of periodicals to keep current and gain professional insights. Also included in many newsletters and journals are classified ads posting job openings.

THE TOP CHIEF EXECUTIVE OFFICERS TODAY

The chief executive officers (CEOs) in large U.S. companies have a number of attributes in common. Roughly two-thirds come from wealthy families or those in which the heads of the households are corporate managers, successful professionals or owners of medium-sized businesses. Most CEOs attended

Ivy League schools such as Yale, Princeton, and Harvard. The next-largest group attended Big Ten schools. Some attended military schools. Almost all hold bachelor degrees. Many have graduate degrees. Most CEOs are married with children. A large number enjoy sports, particularly golf and tennis.

CEOs have come up from a variety of functional areas including finance/accounting, merchandising/marketing, engineering/technical, production/manufacturing, and the legal department. In the past most CEOs have worked for one or two companies. Today there is greater movement from one company to another than ever before as boards attempt to find executives to lead companies through restructuring. *Financial World* magazine named Stanley C. Gault, CEO of The Goodyear Tire & Rubber Company, CEO of the Year. He had successful careers with General Electric and Rubbermaid prior to becoming CEO of Goodyear. Under his leadership the company has profited through increased emphasis on sales, marketing, and customer needs that resulted in the successful introduction of new products like the award-winning Aquatred tire.

The top CEOs are multi-talented, versatile people. This descriptive data offers some insight into those who reach the top of the management pyramid. There is little room at the top, and most new graduates hardly expect to become CEOs of large corporations. Still the backgrounds of these current CEOs give some hints about the types of people who make it to the top.

OPPORTUNITIES FOR MANAGERS

The demand for marketing managers will vary considerably from industry to industry. Business and information services should experience strong growth along with advertising, sales promotion, and public relations agencies. Much of this growth in service agencies is due to outsourcing, a trend among companies to contract work to outside agencies that is likely to continue. This growth will create many new opportunities for marketing managers. The restructuring going on in large corporations will create a demand for product and brand managers to lead marketing teams.

Companies undergoing radical change are firing and retiring managers with old ideas and hiring others to help with the change process. Since the beginning of 1993, IBM has hired over 1300 professionals, including 36 new executives. Executive search firms report record amounts of billings for senior managers and the most active CEO market that they have ever seen. The greatest rise in demand is for marketing executives. One firm reports 35 percent of its searches were for sales and marketing positions, up from the usual 30 percent. Another reported that 45 percent of the positions requested at vice-president levels and above were for senior marketing executives. Marketing executives are considered by some to be the only true generalists in the company with an overall industry perspective. Consequently, they are in great demand even by technology-oriented companies—particularly in the telecommunications and software industries.

MANAGEMENT COMPENSATION

In 1993 Michael D. Eisner, chairman of Walt Disney Co., earned over $203 million, more than any CEO of a public corporation has made in a single year, and more than most make in an entire career. Considering that Disney's total market value has risen from $2.2 billion in 1984 when he took over to $22.7 billion, stockholders aren't complaining. Actually over $202 million resulted from exercising stock options; only $750,000 was salary, putting Eisner at number 188 on a list of 200. Sanford I. Weill, CEO of Travelers Corporation, received the largest compensation package totalling approximately $45,700,000. Total compensation including salary, bonuses, and the present value of stock grants of the 200 highest paid CEOs averaged $4.1 million. The average salary and bonus without stock options and other long-term compensation for all CEOs of major companies was $1,274,893 in 1993, roughly 149 times that of a factory worker.

If you feel "there ought a be a law," be assured that there is one. The federal government has recently put a $1 million cap on corporate deductibility of executive salaries. The irony is that the law established a standard of sorts so that companies that used to pay less than $1 million have raised CEO salaries to that level. Others award higher salaries and suffer the tax consequences, or rather the stockholders suffer the consequences. However, executive compensation is undergoing change. Boards of directors are hiring pay consultants to help determine what their people are worth. A trend to link CEO paychecks to corporate performance has definitely taken hold.

Management compensation varies widely depending on the level of management, length of service, size and location of firm, and scope of responsibility. Figure 8.2, developed from survey results appearing in the February 1994 issue of *Business Marketing*, compares the compensation of vice-presidents in marketing related areas.

Figure 8.2 Compensation of Marketing Vice-presidents

Title	Average base	Average bonus	Average total pay
VP marketing	$126,666	$34,200	$160,866
VP product mgt.	98,269	19,182	117,451
VP brand mgt.	91,875	15,876	107,751
VP advertising	99,761	16,481	116,242

By some estimates women executives in sales and marketing earn roughly 75 percent of the amount their male counterparts earned. However, there is some indication that base salary for women executives is increasing at a faster rate than that of men. Benefits such as stock options and long-term compensation vary greatly as well. Each management position and its compensation package must be evaluated individually. In general, an average salary range for middle-level managers would be from $34,000 to $40,000 plus bonuses. An average salary range for upper-level managers is from $50,000 to $100,000 plus bonuses. More relevant figures for the purposes of this book are the salaries of recent graduates discussed in chapter 11.

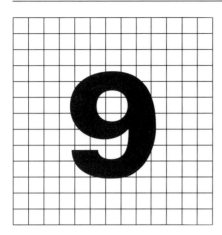

CAREERS IN INTERNATIONAL MARKETING

The next century will witness the full emergence of China as a global trading partner. Recent announcements from China promise the abolition of import quotas and license requirements for 195 types of goods, as reported in The Associated Press. Direct foreign investment is on the rise with fast-growing western economies cashing in on opportunities in developing countries. Money is flowing into China most rapidly. Singapore, Mexico, Argentina, and Malaysia are also major beneficiaries of an influx of foreign capital. India has eased trade restrictions and investors have applied to pump roughly $4 billion in investments into the Indian economy, 40 percent from American companies. U.S. marketers such as RJR Nabisco Inc., Procter & Gamble, Colgate-Palmolive, Johnson & Johnson, and Coca-Cola have entered Russia determined to build brand recognition and consumer loyalty early despite the unrest in the country. The world has truly become a global marketplace.

International marketing, also called global marketing, multinational marketing, and transnational marketing, describes the activities of organizations that engage in exchanges across national boundaries. Both business and non-business organizations such as charities, religious organizations, and universities are involved in international marketing. Whether selling products, soliciting donations, or recruiting students, these organizations operate in a global environment that has its own rules and requirements. Business organizations, whether U.S. based or headquartered abroad, are attempting to tap into the unprecedented growth in international marketing.

THE IMPACT OF FOREIGN COMPETITION ON U.S. CORPORATIONS

Competition from European and Asian markets has forced U.S. companies to think globally and become insiders instead of exporters. The 1992 economic integration of the European Community has removed many trade barriers from country to country. Many U.S. companies in Europe will take advantage of this, including Ford Motor Company, Merck & Company, Coca-Cola Company, IBM, and Hewlett-Packard, all of which have had successful operations in Europe for years. In Japan, McDonald's Corporation, Disney Company, DuPont Company, and Amway have prospered. Nike's U.S. athletic shoe sales have fallen off as American teens and those in their twenties opt for the new look of rugged boots. The economies of Europe and Japan are the key growth markets for that company in the future. The cola wars at home enabled Pepsi to increase domestic market share from 18 to 31 percent. Now Pepsi is moving the battlefield abroad. The biggest lack on Pepsi's part is international executives. Toys 'R' Us, already operating stores in Canada, Europe, Hong Kong, and Singapore, is now open for business in Japan. Though only a limited number of retailers have the kind of format, supplier relationships, and expertise to operate with success globally at this time, this situation is changing rapidly.

The recently revised General Agreement on Tariffs & Trade (GATT) has removed many trade barriers from foreign trade and is expected to lead to the founding of the World Trade Organization. As foreign economies mature, they create huge markets for construction equipment, telecommunications products, and a host of other goods and services. More corporations are building or buying factories in Eastern Europe. The attraction to Eastern Europe is based on its large consumer market and educated labor force. Closer to home, the passage of the North American Free Trade Agreement (NAFTA) with Mexico has wiped out trade barriers such as protective tariffs and moved to create a unified North American economy. While free trade agreements have both positive and negative economic aspects for countries involved, these agreements do change the nature of the global marketplace and create opportunities.

CONSUMER DEMAND AND ITS IMPACT ON GLOBAL MARKETING

The developed areas of the world—Western Europe, Japan, and the U.S.— offer markets for U.S. products, but they are not growing significantly. Consumers in these mature economies have satisfied most of their material needs. However, 77 percent of our global population live in developing countries. Hundreds of millions of consumers in Asia will enter or approach the middle class within the next ten years. They will want to buy a lot of cars, computers, appliances, and televisions. Eastern Europe contains 300 million consumers all needing clothes, appliances, and the most basic items. In South America, an awareness of international brands already exists so the demand is there and the marketing will be easier. This is especially true of the young who watch MTV and sip Coke in great numbers. Those interested in careers in international marketing should broaden their perspective to include preparation to enter these growing markets. Business will follow demand and businesses produce jobs.

HOW COMPANIES ARE INVOLVED IN FOREIGN MARKETS

Foreign Operations and Joint Ventures

Companies have several options for entering foreign markets including foreign operations, joint ventures, exporting, and licensing, as indicated in Figure 9.1. Multinational companies commit a great deal of resources to establishing operations in foreign countries and take on a lot of risk. They run the economic risk of consumers rejecting their product and political risks as well, including confiscation of their property by the government of the host country. To reduce this risk, some companies enter into joint ventures as a way of tapping into foreign markets. The government of the host country or a locally owned firm may go into partnership with a company interested in entering the local market. More and more countries are requiring this type of joint venture as a condition for entering their markets.

Figure 9.1 Options for Foreign Trade

- Foreign Operations
- Joint Ventures
- Exporting
- Licensing

Exporting

An alternative to foreign-based operations is exporting. During the past three years, exports accounted for roughly one-third of U.S. economic growth and are predicted to continue to spur the economy. Exporting accomplishes the objective of selling in foreign markets without the large risk of locating operations in foreign countries. The opening of markets in the East bloc countries along with the increasing demand for U.S. consumer products worldwide has made exporting even more enticing of late. Many companies establish export departments and sell directly to foreign firms. These departments contact foreign buyers, conduct marketing research, and arrange distribution and export documentation. Foreign distribution may be through manufacturers' representatives, import jobbers, dealers, wholesalers, or retailers who function overseas in the same way as their counterparts in the U.S. Their duties are described in chapter 6. As companies become more proficient at exporting, they may begin to explore possibilities for foreign operations. Rather than direct exporting, companies may work through intermediaries. Trading companies are private or government-owned organizations that buy and sell products in much the same way as merchant wholesalers and wholesale dealers/merchandise brokers do. These companies may place orders with exporters for their own accounts or for a client. Some of these companies offer a whole range of services to their clients, including importing, exporting, storing, transporting, and distribution through intermediaries.

One of the biggest headaches small and mid-size exporters have had in the past has been financing. Many banks do not understand the complexities of operating in foreign markets, and those who do are unwilling to spend the hours it takes to set up letters of credit. Regional and foreign-based banks have handled export financing in the past. Today factors, forfaiters, and export trading companies have begun operation to capitalize on the need of exporters to finance their sales and get paid faster. Factors recognize foreign receivables and give the exporter 85 percent of the money owed if the deal is insured by the Export-Import Bank in Washington. Forfaiters accept foreign receivables and give the exporter most of the money before they collect from the buyer when the payment is backed by a government guarantee. Export trading companies take title to the exports and complete the transaction by shipping the goods and collecting payment. These new financial companies who specialize in exports will facilitate more export trade and provide job opportunities themselves.

Foreign Licensing

Still another option, particularly attractive to small companies that cannot afford to invest capital in foreign operations, is foreign licensing. A company will license its concept, which can be a product or a process, to a foreign company that already has facilities and understands the market. In return, the business receives royalties that can range from one-eighth of 1 percent to 15 percent. In addition to royalties, the company may get valuable feedback in research and development and marketing from the foreign licensee.

CAREERS IN INTERNATIONAL MARKETING

Careers in international marketing do not necessarily mean extensive travel. Most multinational companies prefer to fill positions in foreign countries with citizens of that country. The practicality is obvious. Natives speak the language, understand the customs, are paid on a local scale, and do a better job of representing the company than would foreigners. More than likely, graduates in international business, especially at entry-level positions, will be based in the U.S. while dealing with companies abroad. Though lacking in the glamour desired by many young single people, positions in the U.S. do not present such complications as homesickness or education for school-aged children. There are many reasons to enter the field of international marketing, including challenge and growing opportunities. However, it is important to understand that though upper-level managers may be posted abroad or travel abroad frequently, entry- and lower-level personnel will probably be based in the U.S.

Companies based in one country become multinational when they begin to produce and sell goods in other countries. When their operations extend around the world they are referred to as global enterprises. Much groundwork must be done to select and enter foreign markets successfully. The economic, technological, sociocultural, and political environments in which the business must operate differ greatly from country to country, making the activities of international marketing very complex.

International Marketing Research

Although marketing research professionals perform roughly the same duties described in chapter 2, their work is much more complicated. They must first obtain demographic information from secondary sources. Useful data may be obtained from such organizations as the United Nations, the U.N. World Health Organization, the U.N. Food and Agriculture Organization, the Organization for Economic Cooperation and Development, regional trading blocs (e.g., European Community, Association of South East Asian Nations, and Andean Common Market). Governments in foreign countries and U.S. embassies can provide useful information. Researchers also check with non-government sources such as banks, international trade clubs, and executives of companies doing business in the country. However, much of this information may have been estimated or crudely collected and must be carefully analyzed to determine whether or not primary data should be collected.

Collecting primary data is even trickier than analyzing the secondary data. While many marketing research techniques may be adapted for use in developed countries, they may be totally unsuitable for use in developing countries with high illiteracy rates, unreliable postal and telephone service, language barriers, and a general suspicion of people asking a lot of questions. To determine which techniques would be appropriate for use in a country, marketing researchers must be familiar with economic, technological, sociocultural, and political factors within the country. Language skills are invaluable since many sources of information will be in the language of the country.

International Product Management

The product decisions made for products to be marketed abroad are complex. Members of the project management team have three alternatives regarding product development. The least costly is product standardization, where the identical product is sold both at home and abroad. This is only effective if the product is suitable for foreign markets. A second strategy is adaptation, in which a product is modified or adapted to suit local tastes and uses. Finally, product innovation, in which a product is especially designed for each foreign market, is sometimes the best route. The team must also grapple with name, distribution, packaging, pricing, and promotion decisions.

International Promotion

Advertising, sales promotion, publicity, and personal selling must take into account attitudes of consumers, competitors, intermediaries, and governments. Clearly, deciding which approach will be effective and indeed allowed depends on an accurate assessment of these attitudes. Multinational companies can use ad agencies in their home country, local agencies, or a multinational advertising agency with branches in numerous countries. U.S.-based ad agencies have been opening branches in foreign countries for many years. The employees in these branches are hired from the local population. Personal selling is even more culture-bound than advertising. Therefore, sales of consumer products are made by local nationals who understand cultural preferences and etiquette in their country. Many manufacturers of expensive industrial products and pharmaceuticals employ U.S. sales representatives who work abroad; they must study the habits and behaviors of their customers in order to be effective.

OPPORTUNITIES IN INTERNATIONAL MARKETING

Most career opportunities in international marketing exist in the U.S. However, there are some positions abroad for those who have mastered their firm's domestic marketing operations and can speak the language and understand the customs of the country in which they will be based. Opportunities are likely to increase in the future. Travel abroad is usually associated with high-level managers, managers or owners of advertising agencies with operations abroad, owners of export/import businesses, sales representatives of industrial and pharmaceutical products, and fashion coordinators and buyers for stores featuring foreign fashion lines. Positions abroad for recent graduates are very rare, even for those with an MBA and knowledge of a foreign language. Foreign-based jobs may become more plentiful in the future as more corporations create and expand global operations.

Universities are beginning to orient courses toward global marketing and are sponsoring more study abroad. Currently, there are about 1500 overseas-study programs sponsored by U.S. colleges and universities. The Institute of International Study (IIE) publishes *Academic Year Abroad* which describes 2100 programs in over 70 countries that combine travel and study. This publication can be found in libraries or ordered from

> IIE Books
> 809 United Nations Plaza
> New York, NY 10017

Today twenty leading business schools are sending students in their executive MBA programs abroad. Most programs abroad are conducted in partnership with local schools. University of Chicago is the first business school to base an entire executive MBA program abroad. Located in Barcelona, the program is designed to attract managers from all over Europe. Hoping to attract eighty foreign managers a year, University of Chicago will staff the courses with its own Chicago faculty who will research international business problems and take this knowledge back to their students in the U.S. Normally, MBA students are sponsored by their companies who help pay tuition and allow time off from work to attend classes. Job applicants interested in positions abroad should inquire in job interviews about such programs. One study cites that eight out of ten international employees working abroad work for small firms. That trend will continue; those seeking international work should investigate opportunities with small companies.

AISEC, a student-run, nonprofit organization, helps to set up foreign internships abroad for American students wanting international experience. Students live and work in a foreign country as part of exchange programs that last from six weeks to eighteen months. Students interested in international marketing should become proficient in a language and systematically collect information on countries and industries of interest. The annual *Directory of Overseas Summer Jobs* published by Peterson's Guides, Inc. is a useful resource found in some libraries and career centers.

Opportunities are increasing for recent graduates who would like to work in Japan, but candidates must be fluent in Japanese and have a technical skill. DISCO International Career Resources, a subsidiary of a Japanese search firm based in Boston, helped Japanese companies recruit 130 students through job fairs. The demand for Americans to work in Asia is predicted to rise in the future because of the lack of universities in nations such as Malaysia, Taiwan, and South Korea to educate sufficient numbers of technical workers.

SOURCES OF INFORMATION

Those who are interested in international marketing can gain more information about the field from international marketing associations such as those listed below:

American Association of Exporters and Importers
11 West Forty-second Street
New York, NY 10036
(212)944-2230

International Trade Club of Chicago
203 North Wabash Avenue, Suite 1102
Chicago, IL 60601
(312)368-9197

International Trade Council
3114 Circle Hill Road
Alexandria, VA 22305
(703)548-1234

International Traders Association
c/o The Mellinger Company
6100 Variel Avenue
Woodland Hills, CA 91367
(818)884-4400

World Trade Center of New Orleans
2 Canal Street, Suite 2900
New Orleans, LA 70130
(504)529-1601

Several directories offer information on companies doing business abroad, including *Directory of European Retailers*, *Directory of American Firms Operating in Foreign Countries*, *Directory of Foreign Firms Operating in the U.S.*, *Principal International Businesses*, and *The World Marketing Directory*. In addition, Surrey Books, Inc. has published *How to Get a Job in Europe* by Robert Sanborn, which lists over 2000 employers in thirty-five countries. This book is part of a series that offers information on jobs in the Pacific Rim and in various cities around the U.S. Another publication, *The Almanac of International Jobs and Careers* by Ronald L. Krannick and Caryl Rae Krannick gives information on organizations abroad that hire U.S. citizens.

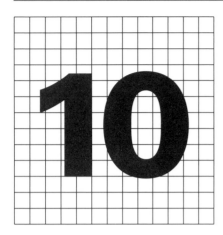

CAREERS IN EDUCATION, CONSULTING, AND ENTREPRENEURSHIP

Working in a large corporate environment is not for everyone. Some people are mavericks who require greater autonomy in a work atmosphere. A marketing background often leads individuals to pursue careers in higher education, consulting, or entrepreneurship. A recent survey of senior business majors at a large eastern university showed that most respondents considered operating one's own business to be the best means to attain their goals. However, when asked to consider what their realistic choice would be, only five percent felt that they would actually operate their own businesses. The careers described in this chapter are not for beginners but can be viable goals with the proper education and experience. Most successful entrepreneurs have worked for others and gained important knowledge and skills before striking out on their own. This chapter will explore some interesting career alternatives.

MARKETING EDUCATION

Graduate Degree Requirements

Professional educators in the field of marketing find positions in two- and four-year colleges with marketing courses or programs of study. A master's degree in marketing is usually sufficient qualification to find a teaching position in a community college. Depending on supply and demand, a doctorate might be required and is always preferred. A doctorate in marketing is always required for tenure-track positions in four-year colleges and universities. Earning one's doctorate requires a large commitment of both time and money. After a four-year bachelor's program, a master's program requiring at least two years of full-time study must be undertaken. Successful completion of a master-level program does not guarantee admission to a doctoral program.

Applicants must not only have the ability to successfully complete graduate courses in marketing, but they must achieve a certain score on the Graduate Management Admissions Test (GMAT) and demonstrate the potential for conducting original research. Doctoral programs require at least two years of full-time coursework and seminars along with the design and completion of a doctoral dissertation. This can be a lengthy process, and each step must be approved by a committee before the candidate may go on. A review of the literature, design of the project, data gathering or laboratory experimentation, and an analysis of results can take well over a year to complete.

The reputation of the university and its doctoral program along with the student's assigned major professor are factors that come into play when recent doctoral recipients apply to prestigious and well-known universities. Therefore, those seeking doctorates should carefully evaluate a school and its program before entering. Finding a major professor who shares a student's research interests and who is well known in the field can make doctoral study easier and more valuable. It can also make the student more marketable when entering the job market.

As the demand for marketing professionals increases, so increases the demand for marketing educators. Demand may vary with area of specialization. Doctoral candidates may concentrate in marketing research, marketing management, purchasing, and so forth. Recent graduates are considered for positions as instructors or assistant professors. Selection criteria can include dissertation and other research, publications, evaluations of professors, and experience outside the doctoral program such as previous employment in marketing areas. In addition, teaching evaluations may be considered since most doctoral students teach undergraduate marketing classes as part of their graduate assistantships.

Responsibilities and Advancement

Instructors in two-year schools teach primarily but may be expected to write books and articles as well. University professors normally have lighter teaching loads but are required to publish articles in their field in order to be considered for promotion and tenure. In addition, both instructors and professors are evaluated on service to their schools, which usually includes serving on committees and can involve fund-raising. Assistant professors are promoted to associate professor, then full professor. Often college professors enter administrative positions such as marketing department chairman or dean. Posts such as dean of undergraduate or graduate business studies or dean of the college of business administration (as well as other deanships on a college campus) are sometimes filled by former marketing professors. Figure 10.1 shows the organization of a typical university college of business. It is not unusual for professors to earn money outside the university as

Figure 10.1 University College of Business Hierarchy

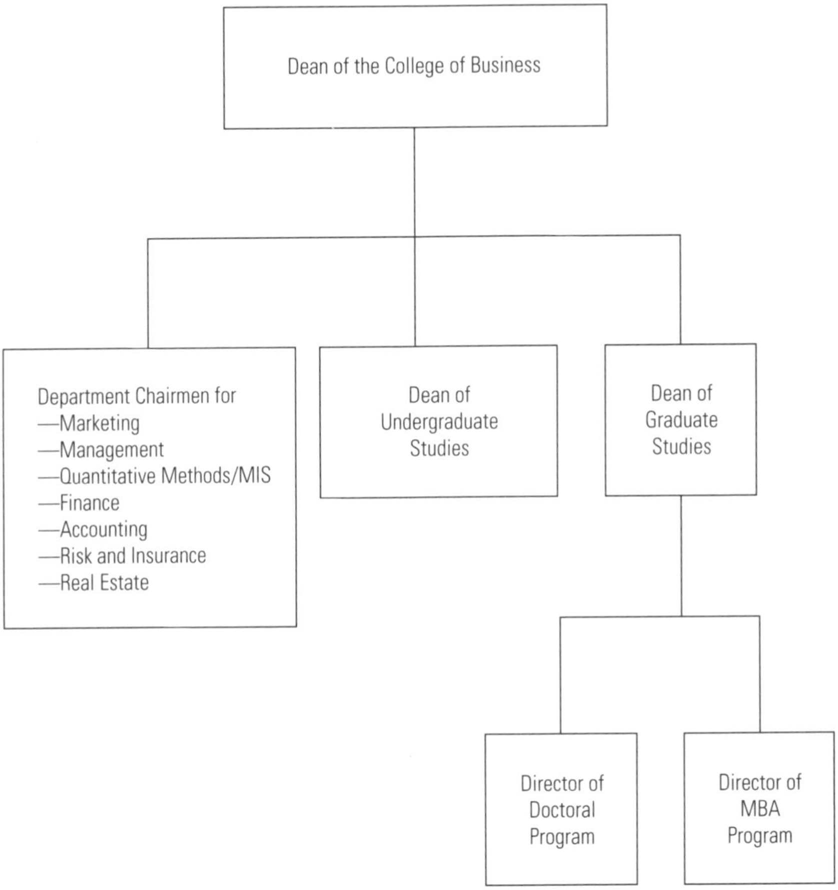

consultants and sometimes entrepreneurs. Super Lube, the rapidly growing quick oil change franchise, was started by two Florida State University professors—one in marketing and one in real estate.

MARKETING CONSULTING

In 1993 AT&T spent $347.1 million on consulting and research services acquired from nearly 1000 consulting firms. The biggest recipients were such firms as McKinsey & Company, Monitor Company, and Arthur Andersen. As companies grow, shrink, restructure, and begin global operations, they are employing consultants in record numbers to help with these transitions. In 1993 alone over 80,000 consultants, some with huge global companies and others working from their basements, did $17 billion worth of business, according to a *Business Week* July 25, 1994, article.

Marketing consultants are problem solvers who have extensive experience in marketing and an area of expertise, such as marketing strategy, marketing research, advertising, sales, or merchandising. Business and industry hire consultants to help plan marketing strategies and solve problems when strategies go awry. Consulting firms and independent consultants in the U.S. and Canada are listed in *Consultants and Consulting Organizations Directory* found in the reference section of libraries. Companies hire marketing consultants mostly in the areas of marketing strategy, market and product research, and feasibility studies.

What Consultants Do

Since consultants work for many clients, they are exposed to different methods of solving problems and a variety of valuable sources of information. Consultants use their diverse experiences to analyze and solve problems for clients. Having a knowledge of what works and what doesn't work in a variety of situations, the consultant can make recommendations that can save time and money. Most consultants have tremendous freedom over their time and other resources. Whether they freelance, work in small companies, or work for large consulting firms, they work independently with their individual clients. In order to be rehired by a client, a consultant must demonstrate the ability to help solve the client's problems in both creative and cost-effective ways. Consulting is not the job for someone who wants to work less and avoid the nine-to-five routine. Longer though less routine hours are required for successful consulting. Often client companies impose difficult-to-meet deadlines and expect unrealistic results.

Trends in Consulting

Change management and corporate reengineering are the hot areas in the consulting business today. After reengineering in the U.S. is complete, there will be Europe to reengineer, and after that corporations around the rest of the globe. Once consultant work was narrow in scope and the consultant worked alone. Today, consultants team up with managers and work together to analyze and solve problems. Companies in the process of down-sizing management positions have begun to use consultants to complete projects that previously would have been done in-house. Short-term assignments have given way to projects lasting years and involving crucial strategy, operations, organization, and technology management. Consultants are working on longer assignments, and companies are paying higher fees. However, executives are expecting more for their money in terms of positive results.

Finding Clients

A consultant competes with other consultants for jobs. Though the use of consultants may greatly benefit a business, it is not required for doing business and is one of the first budget items to be cut in hard times. Therefore, consultants must sell their services aggressively. Consultants use a number of promotional techniques to obtain clients: personal relationships and networking, participation in seminars, mailing and phoning, door-to-door selling, advertising, marketing agents, and public relations companies.

Unless a company is rehiring a consultant who has worked for it previously, the company will usually screen and interview a number of consultants. For large contracts, company representatives will visit recent client sites and ask for evidence that the consultant produced results. Who is hired depends on a number of factors. The first is how well the company managers and consultant get along personally since they will usually be working together as a team. The quality of the consultant's references, including companies (probably not competitors) for whom the consultant has completed an assignment similar to the one proposed, is another primary consideration. Although consultants may work for competing companies, often consulting contracts stipulate that they may not disclose privileged company information or work for a competing firm for a certain time period. Finally, the number of years of experience and the quality of that experience are considered.

Sometimes consultants hire consulting broker firms to locate clients. Brokers normally earn 25 to 40 percent of what the consultant earns on the initial contact with the hiring company and less on subsequent contacts. Consulting fees vary greatly depending on the scope and complexity of the project and the reputation of the consultant. Well-established, successful consultants rarely want for employment. Building a reputation as a consultant requires hard work over a number of years.

Working for a Consulting Firm

Because people are the greatest resource in consulting companies, everyone in large consulting companies gets involved in recruiting new employees. In general, consultants enter the field with two to four years of experience and a college degree, often an MBA or doctorate. Top consulting firms hire graduates from the best business schools and then train them. These firms also offer summer internships to promising candidates and evaluate these recruits before offering them permanent employment with the firm.

Work in large consulting firms is characterized by pressure, long hours, travel, and high turnover. These firms are partnerships that follow an up-or-out policy; that is, consultants have from five to seven years to make partner. If they fail, they are out. Only one in five who begin work with a large company are expected to make partner. Many opt for consulting with large firms for the training and experience, then go out on their own by choice. Most consulting firms are based in the Northeast and California. Larger firms have branches throughout the country.

Companies often retain consultants on a continuing basis, so consulting work tends to be long term. Entry-level consulting work in large companies is primarily research. As junior consultants or associates demonstrate the analytic, interpersonal, and motivational skills required for success in the job, they are promoted to the position of case team leader or senior consultant. In this capacity, a consultant supervises a small team normally working on one or two cases at a time. Three or four years later, if the senior consultant is performing well, he or she is promoted to consulting manager. As manager, a consultant leads a consulting team on important client projects. Once promoted to junior partner and finally senior partner or director, the consultant's work is primarily marketing the firm and its services. Figure 10.2 shows a career path in a large consulting firm.

Though beginners may be hired out of college with undergraduate marketing degrees, an MBA is required by most firms for advancement. Most beginners earn $28,000 to $34,000 a year with mid- and end-of-year bonuses. College graduates with two years of experience can earn approximately $50,000 plus bonuses. MBAs earn salaries in the range of $45,000 to $90,000. Competition is heating up among large consulting firms in recruiting top graduates. Recently, a top MBA graduate was offered a $95,000 base salary, a $20,000 signing bonus, and a fully loaded laptop computer. Beginning consultants with MBAs from top business schools such as Harvard and Stanford earn $60,000 plus bonuses. Salaries increase dramatically with promotions. Junior partners earn in excess of $150,000 plus bonuses and shares in the firm. Senior partners earn from $300,000 to $600,000, with the most senior earning salaries in excess of $1 million.

Independent Consulting The number of small consulting operations with no more than three people has doubled between 1991 and 1993. Estimates are that only one in five will succeed. Success will depend in part on how well consultants can use the new technology, especially electronic networks, to gain information. Independent consulting may be done on a full-time or part-time basis. Many university professors consult to supplement their university salaries. Retired executives or executives between jobs are in demand as consultants. A marketing-strategy consultant should have been employed as a successful marketing manager in a position fairly high up in an organization before seeking independent status. Although consultants are well-paid *when* they work, paying the bills requires steady work. Self-employed consultants must earn 50 percent more than their large-firm counterparts to pay for the costs of doing business and the benefits normally provided by the company such as health insurance, paid holidays and vacations, travel expenses, office space, supplies and equipment, clerical help, and telephone expenses.

Many consultants are corporate drop-outs. Kim T. Gordon quit her job as marketing vice-president of a large real estate sales company to start her home-based business, Marketing and Communications Counsel. Gordon offers strategic planning services in marketing and communications. In her first year of business, she earned $15,000 more than she earned working for someone else. Gordon has total control over her time and her business. Although the business is growing, she wants to continue to run it from her home—an opportunity made possible by computer technology and other electronic tools.

Figure 10.2 Career Path in a Large Consulting Firm

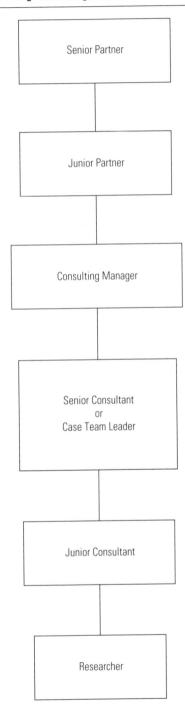

Sources of Information for Consultants

Numerous publications are available to those interested in consulting as a profession. Consultants are listed in a number of directories, including *Dun's Consultant's Directory* and *Consultants and Consulting Organizations Directory*, found in the reference section of the library. *Consultants News* and *Journal of Management Consulting* are periodicals covering up-to-date information in the field. Some associations for consultants are listed below:

American Consultants League
1290 Palm Avenue
Sarasota, FL 34236
(813)952-9290

American Association of Professional Consultants
9140 Ward Parkway
Kansas City, MO 64114
(913)681-3242

Council of Consulting Organizations
521 5th Avenue, Thirty-fifth Floor
New York, NY 10175-3598
(212)697-9693

Professional and Technical Consultants Association
P.O. Box 4143
Mountain View, CA 94040
(415)903-8305

ENTREPRENEURSHIP

Last year more people were involved in starting their own businesses than were getting married or having babies. Over two million new businesses were formed in 1993, 20 percent of which were one or two person operations. Some new business start-ups were by those who lost their jobs as a result of downsizing, but most were by individuals seeking a better quality of life than they are able to find working for someone else. This new generation of entrepreneurs is better educated and is starting with more sophisticated businesses than previous groups. Many of their companies provide consulting or business services to other businesses, using affordable, powerful computers and telecommunications equipment.

Small businesses account for about half of the nonfarm, nongovernmental employment in the U.S. Over the past six years, they have generated about 44 million jobs. About five percent of the small businesses create most of the jobs. However, apart from job creation, entrepreneurial companies spur large ones to make innovations in products and to create new markets. Consider the impact on technology made by Bill Gates and the impact on retailing made by Sam Walton, that five-and-dime store manager from Arkansas. Realistically, most of today's small businesses provide only a modest living for their owners. The majority will go out of business within the first three years.

Entrepreneurs are those individuals who are willing to assume the risks of starting their own businesses. Given this risk, which is considerable, why do they do it? A survey of almost 3000 business owners was conducted by Arnold C. Cooper of Purdue University. Respondents identified these reasons as very important in the following order: to use my skills or ability, to gain control over my life, to build for the family, for the challenge, to live how or where I like, to gain respect or recognition, to earn lots of money, to fulfill other's expectations, as the best alternative available. Women have been starting businesses at twice the rate of men. More African-Americans are starting their own companies. A black business network of powerful contacts is helping to drive economic growth in such areas as communications, entertainment, and consumer goods.

Entrepreneurs Start with a Good Idea

The demand for a product or service creates an opportunity for prospective entrepreneurs. Understanding that consumers in the 1990s want to be educated, entertained, preserve the environment, be good parents, stay healthy, and feel rich, clever entrepreneurs are designing products to meet these needs. Big business leaves many needs unmet and market niches untapped. Walter Hudson, weighing in at 1400 pounds, recognized a need for large clothes so he began Walter Hudson Ventures, a mail-order firm that sells designer clothes to women weighing from 200 to 1000 pounds. Sally Fox, a hand-spinner and weaver, found a paper bag containing brown cotton seeds and lint while working for a cotton breeder. She identified a market for natural, undyed brown cotton and started Natural Cotton Colours, Inc. One of six children, Daniel Lauer and his siblings created many of their own toys. His recollection of his sisters filling rubber gloves and balloons with water, painting faces on them, and dressing them up gave him the idea for WaterBabies. Only about 100 of the 5000 to 6000 toys introduced each year are successful. Entrepreneurs go against the odds every time they start a new business, but that doesn't stop many from succeeding.

Independent entrepreneurs find a market niche, develop a product, and market it as do large companies. For example, Richard Worth capitalized on the public's interest in nutrition by selling "healthy" jam, followed by "healthy" cookies. His company R.W. Frookies, sells whole-grain cookies sweetened with fruit juice. While employed as a marketing consultant, Worth and his wife, a nutritionist, put their heads together and developed recipes and a business plan. He raised money from suppliers and distributors to begin the company. In two years his company went from zero to $18 million in sales. This was not accomplished through luck. A tremendous amount of knowledge and tireless effort are required to develop a successful small business.Worth still works from twelve to sixteen hours a day—the norm for successful small business owners. Speaking of cookies, Debbi Fields opened her first store in 1977 at age 20 with a $50,000 loan from a banker who liked her chocolate chip cookies. Ten years later Mrs. Fields Inc. was a company of 543 stores in six countries, including Japan and Australia.

Succeeding as an Entrepreneur

Because of the large investment of time and money and the high risk of failure, an entrepreneur must have a total commitment to the business, a tolerance for hard work, good health, and financial backing. The prospective entrepreneur usually seeks financial backing from relatives, friends, and lending institutions. Normally entrepreneurs put a good bit of their own money into their businesses. If they have developed an impressive business plan, they may be successful in getting financial backing from outside sources such as banks or venture capitalists. Venture capital firms are usually groups of investors who extend financial backing annually to 30,000 to 40,000 start-up companies in return for part ownership of the company, depending on the terms of each arrangement. Usually the venture capital firm wants to protect its investment by having considerable say in how the company is run. Many small business owners have taken on the risk of starting their own businesses in order to have total freedom to run them as they see fit. When this is the case, the entrepreneur attempts to go it alone, avoiding capital with strings attached.

While securing financial backing is often the stumbling block beyond which hopeful entrepreneurs cannot go, more than money is required to make a business thrive. Once finances are secured, an entrepreneur begins to implement the business plan. Since in most small businesses, the owner is responsible for planning, accounting, purchasing, producing, marketing, staffing, and overall management, a general knowledge of all the activities of business is required. Above all, an entrepreneur must be a salesperson extraordinaire—first selling the idea in order to raise the capital to start the company, then selling the company and its future to prospective employees, and finally selling the product to consumers who are constantly bombarded with ideas for new and better products. Entrepreneurs should be very aware of market and economic conditions if they hope to succeed, and these conditions are constantly changing.

Preparing for Entrepreneurship

Can a person be taught to be an entrepreneur? Probably not. But what can be taught are the skills needed for an entrepreneur to be successful. Because of demand, business schools are adding more courses and encouraging more student participation in entrepreneurial competitions. Almost 100 schools offer comprehensive entrepreneurship programs usually in the form of a concentration of electives. Coursework focuses on the financing of a new business and the commercialization of new products. The turbulent job market has propelled many recent graduates into starting businesses. The best preparation, however, is outside the classroom, working for a company in the same industry that the prospective entrepreneur would like to enter.

Larry Villella, at age 11, started his own company. In charge of watering the lawn, he hated moving the sprinkler around tree trunks and shrubs so he invented a C-shaped sprinkler to fit around them. His company, ConServ Products Company, grossed about $70,000 in its first four years. A study of 685 preschoolers revealed qualities such as a taste for risk taking, a talent for creative problem solving, and high achievement motivation. According to Marilyn Kourilsky who conducted the study, potential entrepreneurs are selling lemonade or something else by the time they enter school. Participation in organizations such as Junior Achievement, Future Business Leaders of America, or Entrecon at Wharton can help kindle that entrepreneurial fire in many young people.

Parents can play a role in encouraging their children to be creative and entrepreneurial. Karen Davis wanted her daughters Tonia, age 10, and Jesse, age 11, to learn about business so she helped them start the Davis Baking Co. They designed a marketing brochure, placed it in mailboxes in their small town, and baked cookies as the orders came in. The first summer the company netted $700 after expenses. Jesse sold her share of the business to Tonia for $120. Tonia showed a flair for marketing by sending a brochure to parents of children who planned to attend a nearby camp offering to deliver fresh-baked cookies to camp. That summer Tonia netted $2400, bought a computer, invested $1200 in the Pioneer International Growth Fund, and made a contribution to a rain forest protection group. This year the company expanded its product offering, mailed out 10,000 brochures, bought a computer program to track orders, installed an 800 number for credit card orders, and hired a professional baker. Tonia has given 50 percent of the company to her mother in exchange for all her time and help, retained a 50 percent interest herself, and removed herself from company operations but signed on as a consultant for the summer of 1995. And that is how it is done!

Sources of Information for Small Businesses

Usually small family businesses employ family members in key positions and, if the business has a board of directors, they are often family members. In such a situation, the question of where to get objective advice on business matters arises. The Small Business Administration (SBA), with offices in all major cities, is an excellent source of information for those who want to start their own businesses or need help once they have set up shop. Numerous brochures published by SBA are available in SBA offices around the country or may be requested by mail. These brochures give valuable how-to information on developing a business plan, acquiring financing, marketing products, and much more. Many books have been written on managing small businesses. Small business consultants offer services to small business owners who can afford them. A source of advice for businesses with annual revenues of at least $2 million and at least twenty-five employees is a San Diego-based company called Executive Committee Inc., which organizes conferences for groups of executives from small companies. These meetings consist of a presentation by a business expert and a problem-solving session during which the executives help one another find solutions to problems. Membership in an executive group is by invitation and costs $7,600 per year.

Information and assistance for small business owners can be obtained by writing some of the following:

Chamber of Commerce of the United States
1615 H Street, N.W.
Washington, DC 20062-2000
(202)659-6000

National Association of Small Business Investment Companies
1199 North Fairfax Street, Suite 200
Alexandria, VA 22314
(703)683-1601

National Association of Women Business Owners
1010 Wayne Avenue, Suite 900
Silver Spring, MD 20910
(301)608-2596

National Federation of Independent Business
53 Century Boulevard, Suite 300
Nashville, TN 37214
(615)872-5800

SWAP Club International
P.O. Box 149
Arvada, CO 80001
(303)534-4937

U.S. Small Business Administration
1441 L Street, N.W.
Washington, DC 20416

FRANCHISE OWNERSHIP

Many people who want to own a small businesses, but have neither an original idea nor the business acumen to start a business from scratch, choose to buy a franchise. A franchise is an agreement between a small business owner and a parent company that gives the owner the right to sell the company's product (goods or services) under conditions agreed upon by both. The store itself is also called a franchise. A great many small retail stores are franchises, including fast-food stores, gas stations, print shops, and others selling almost every type of good or service. Statistics show that the proportionate number of failures among franchises is significantly less than failures among small businesses in general. The reason for this difference is that franchises enjoy special advantages over other small business operations.

Advantages to Franchise Ownership

Failure among franchises is reduced by the nature of the franchise itself. Franchises sell nationally known and extensively tested products for which a market has already been established. Training and assistance from the parent company help the new owner choose a location, set up shop, estimate potential sales, and design market strategies that have worked in similar locations. Cooperative buying power enables the franchise owner to purchase supplies at lower costs from distributors supplying all franchises of the parent company. Sometimes the parent company helps the new franchise establish credit; this is helpful because it usually takes a new business at least six months to turn a profit. Often this period is longer; sometimes a business is never profitable. Even franchises of a successful parent company sometimes fail.

Disadvantages to Franchise Ownership

Franchise owners pay a franchising fee plus a percentage of their profits to the parent company. This percentage is determined by the amount of advertising and consulting support given by the parent company and varies considerably. It can range from 3 percent to a whopping 50 percent in the temporary-help business. However, in the temporary-help business, the franchisor finances the payrolls of the franchisees. The requirement that the owner buy both equipment and supplies from vendors specified by the parent company may prevent the franchise owner from making more economical purchases elsewhere.

Before entering into an agreement, a business owner should read the fine print and get legal advice as well. The law requires that franchisors must provide a detailed franchise prospectus to potential franchisees. It is wise to keep in mind that the business of the franchise parent company is selling franchises, and like all businesses, it is going to make the product as appealing as possible. The potential profits as well as estimated costs of setting up the franchise stated by the parent company should be assessed by questioning other franchise owners as well as objective sources. The Federal Trade Commission requires that franchisors divulge any litigation in which they are involved. Because fraudulent claims and franchise scams are on the rise, a franchise agreement should be entered into carefully and with legal advice and as much outside knowledge of the parent company as possible.

Growth in Franchises

More then one-third of retail dollars are spent in franchised businesses today, and predictions are that more than half of all retail sales in the 1990s will be generated by franchises. Although such mainstream franchises as hotels, fast-food restaurants, and car-rental agencies have reached a saturation point, new opportunities in business and professional services are available. Manufacturers are franchising aspects of the distribution process such as sales territories and delivery routes in order to reduce overhead. More franchise opportunities will be available partially because it costs less for a company to franchise than it did fifteen years ago. Uniform disclosure documents are accepted in all states, reducing legal fees.

From the standpoint of the franchisee, most franchises cost from $50,000 to $250,000, with the average being $140,000. Home-based franchises can run as little as $10,000. The most expensive franchises can cost as much as $10 million. The percentage of these costs required in cash varies with current credit conditions and ranges from 20 percent to 40 percent. The remaining amount can be bank-financed or pledged with personal guarantees and collateral. Franchise agreements are not to be entered into lightly. The monetary cost of failure can be considerable.

The failure rate for franchises is estimated at about 10 percent per year. This figure includes both franchises that go out of business and those who have been bought out by the franchisor or another franchisee. Franchises fail for many reasons. Lack of financing to support the business until it becomes profitable may cause failure. Even with services and training provided by the franchisor, some owners simply lack the skills required to run a successful business. Often investors buy franchises and hire others to run them. Incentives are different for paid employees than for owners. Thus lack of involvement by the investor is often cited as the major reason for business failure. Sometimes the parent company fails, causing all franchisees to shut down—successful or not.

Boston Chicken, the star of the franchise world, plans to open one store every business day this year. Grow Biz, with 583 stores, mostly franchised, plans to open 200 more this year with 90 percent of the new franchise owners coming from corporate middle-management jobs. Experts were asked to predict tomorrow's successes, and this is what they came up with: better tasting bagels; business services such as postal centers, temporary job agencies, and travel agencies; fast food in Eastern Europe; buffet-style dining; home-based services such as mobile dry cleaning and mobile auto detailing; and the information superhighway because someone is bound to figure out how to sell a franchise.

Sources of Information on Franchises

The growth of franchising can be seen in *Entrepreneur* magazine's annual Franchise 500 issues, which lists 873 franchisors. The *Franchise Opportunities Handbook* published by the Bureau of Industrial Economics and Minority Business Development Agency of the U.S. Department of Commerce can be found in the government documents section of most libraries. Published monthly, it includes a list of franchises for sale as well as excellent tips for prospective franchise owners, a checklist for evaluating a franchise, financial assistance information, and a bibliography of sources of franchising information. Other sources include the following:

> *Directory of Franchise Business Opportunities*
> Franchise Business Opportunities Publishing Company
> 1725 Washington Road, Suite 205
> Pittsburgh, PA 15241

> *Directory of Franchising Organizations*
> Pilot Industries, Inc.
> 347 Fifth Avenue
> New York, NY 10016

> *The Franchise Annual*
> Info Press
> 736 Center Street
> Lewiston, NY 14092

> International Franchise Association
> 1350 New York Avenue, N.W.
> Suite 900
> Washington, D.C. 20005
> (202)628-8000

The directories listed above are revised annually and provide information on many franchise opportunities. These franchises should be investigated thoroughly by contacting both the Better Business Bureau and the International Franchise Association. Many excellent books on franchising are on the market, a number of them available through the International Franchise Association itself.

TRENDS IN THE JOB MARKET

Between now and the year 2005, there will be on average 320,000 openings for college graduates. This figure is much larger than the past decade because of the openings created by the aging of the college-educated workforce. Understanding trends in the job market is particularly important for entry-level job seekers. Major transformations have occurred in American business over the past two decades that affect marketing careers, including the shift to a service economy, the globalization of business, the restructuring of corporations, the impact of technology, the diversification in the workforce, and changing lifestyles of American families. These transformations affect the types of products offered, the nature of jobs involved in marketing them, the demand for individuals with certain skills, the salaries offered workers, even the sizes and locations of businesses themselves.

Throughout this book, trends related to specific fields were highlighted, salaries and demand statistics cited, and opportunities for individuals in certain areas discussed. This chapter will deal with a larger perspective to facilitate a comparison of job opportunities across the field of marketing.

SERVICES MARKETING

We live in a service-oriented economy. Roughly 75 percent of all jobs are in a service industry. It is likely that this percentage will rise even higher. New college graduates in the 1990s will find most opportunities in such fields as health care services, convention planning, financial services, and others that they may have never considered or know very little about. To better understand marketing opportunities in the service industries, it is necessary to differentiate between a good and a service from a marketing perspective. A service is an activity performed for an individual or a firm. While a physical product is impersonal, a service is highly personal. Its quality is contingent on the performance of the worker and can vary considerably within a firm.

Service marketers direct and implement a service firm's marketing effort. Using marketing researchers to determine the needs of its chosen market and the price customers will pay for the firm's service, service marketers function much like any marketing manager. Service industries may be equipment-based, people-based, or a combination of both. For example, electronic databases, automated bank tellers, and diagnostic medical equipment are the tools of equipment-based service industries. An advertising agency is people-based. Only by motivating and inspiring people can managers assure that the service rendered is top quality.

Marketing services is considerably more challenging than marketing goods. Services are intangible. Banks and airlines cannot give samples or claim qualities that outlast those of the competition. Services go out of existence as they are created. They cannot be repossessed if bills are unpaid. Although services cannot be stored as inventory, they must be produced on demand. Long lines or an inability to accommodate customers can seriously impair a service business. Services cannot be mailed; they must be delivered on the spot at a convenient location. Quality is very hard to control—similar services can vary greatly from organization to organization, employee to employee, and even for the same employee. Everyone has bad days. These unique aspects of services require attention and focus by the marketers in a service industry.

In human-intensive services such as advertising and consulting, the employees are the assets. Service sales representatives perform the same activities as those selling goods, as discussed in chapters 6 and 7. An important distinction is that service companies gain much of their business through referrals from satisfied customers. A retail store selling goods might lose some business if a salesperson is rude or incompetent. If it is a specialty shop, a customer might return but avoid the particular salesperson. In a service business, the service itself is the product. A customer receiving poor service will not return and will share the dissatisfaction with others. The success of the service firm depends on hiring the best employees. The pressure to deliver high quality service is intense.

Most new college graduates will be employed in service industries. Experts predict continuing high demand for services sales representatives. It is important to identify an industry as well as a field and prepare oneself for its unique demands. Areas where demand will be particularly strong for sales representatives are temporary help services, business and financial services, information services, and advertising sales. Hotel and automotive service sales will also grow at a faster-than-average rate. Competition among professional service firms is affecting hiring practices. More of these companies are hiring marketing directors, coordinators, and business development personnel. The professional service marketing job responsibilities include research, coordinating seminars, and writing brochures.

The following are associations for individuals in the business and professional services industry.

Professional Services Management Association
4726 Park Road, Suite A
Charlotte, NC 28209
(704)521-8890

Society for Marketing Professional Services
99 Canal Center Plaza, Suite 250
Alexandria, VA 22314
(703)549-6117

THE RESTRUCTURING OF AMERICAN CORPORATIONS

The 1980s were a turbulent period in American business causing major restructuring in corporations, much of which continues in the 1990s. Acquisitions and buyouts changed many corporate identities. Recession and competition from abroad forced downsizing and restructuring. Assigning limited resources in a vastly more complex marketplace is the challenge confronting managers in the 1990s. The business environment of the next decade will be characterized by an uncertain economy, more global competition, shortened product life cycles, and customers demanding better quality and more convenience. The reduction in numbers of midlevel managers, as described in chapter 8, is good news and bad news. First the bad news: Advancement in the corporate hierarchy will become increasingly competitive, and most college graduates will remain in the same jobs for longer periods of time, perhaps five years instead of the two years spent in the same position by the upwardly mobile of the 1970s. Also fewer types of positions will be available to new graduates. Now the good news: Even entry-level jobs will be more varied and challenging. Managers with too much to do will be forced to delegate many tasks to lower-level and beginning employees. Project teams will be more widely used as companies attempt a more entrepreneurial approach to product development. Work will be less structured. More freedom, as a result of reduced numbers of supervisors, will enable employees to show what they are able to do.

Marketing is a line function, that is, marketing activities result in sales and profit; therefore, marketing will get the lion's share of the available resources. Public relations (PR), however, is not always considered a marketing activity and is regarded as a staff function; that is, one that supports line functions. PR will be affected more adversely by budget cuts than other marketing activities. The downsizing of staffs within different departments will contribute to the trend of outsourcing, or contracting out certain types of work. Often outsourcing is more cost effective than maintaining specialized departments and staff. Contracting out advertising, sales promotion, and public relations campaigns will become more common, which is good news for the firms offering these services. Marketing and economic research and consulting firms will be positively affected by this trend. The use of companies providing information processing services will greatly increase. Therefore, many opportunities of the next decade will be with new businesses providing these types of services.

THE IMPACT OF CHANGING TECHNOLOGY

Advances in information and communications technology have revolutionized the workplace of today and created opportunities for companies and individuals that simply did not exist a mere decade ago. Computers are faster, cheaper, smaller, and infinitely more versatile than ever before. New technology has enabled managers to make better decisions faster. Computers perform sophisticated marketing research analysis, such as multivariate statistical analyses, that is too complex to do manually. Monitoring the economic and business environments is easier. Advances in manufacturing equipment allow managers to respond more rapidly to competition, and improved distribution and inventory techniques make sales campaigns more efficient and effective. Improved graphics technology has greatly affected the field of advertising. Breakthroughs in telecommunications technology have furthered the development of branch or satellite offices and the expansion of global operations. In short, technological change has dramatically affected every aspect of marketing.

CHANGES IN LIFESTYLES AND VALUES

Individual lifestyles and values have been changing over the years. More and more people are viewing work as a way to maintain lifestyle rather than developing lifestyles consistent with work. The family is taking central importance in the choices people make, both in their careers and as consumers. People are marrying and having children later in life when careers are already in place. Thus, in an ever-increasing number of two-career couples, both partners are beginning to share in family responsibilities. Though studies show that it is still the woman who misses work most frequently when children are ill, men are definitely doing more of the shopping. In addition, the divorce rate is decreasing.

Lifestyle considerations have caused individuals to place greater emphasis on the quality of life. Many professionals start their own businesses for both personal and professional reasons. Women with children often work or run their own businesses at home. Working at home, or telecommuting, is possible for many employed by companies through information and communications technology. Working part-time is an option for many.

Contingent workers are self-employed or work part-time and include those who do not work forty hours a week, year-round, for the same employer.

They include a wide variety of workers such as part-time clerks, movie stars, or self-employed doctors and make up, by some counts, 30 percent of the work force. This flexible source of labor makes U.S. business more efficient than its European competitors. Of the roughly 35 million contingent workers, almost 11 million are self-employed by choice or profession. More than 17 million of the 22 million part-time workers do so by choice as well. The other 5 million would like full-time employment.

SUPPLY AND DEMAND PROJECTIONS

Overall, the demand for business and management majors has been consistently strong. In the areas of sales and marketing demand has increased particularly for business-to-business marketers. High-tech knowledge is very much in demand in all areas today and will improve a beginner's chances of getting a good job. The increased number of recruiters on college campuses signals increased demand and will greatly help new graduates in their job search. Over half of the job offers are within the service sector; this number is continuing to increase. Other percentage increases in offers have come from public accounting, merchandising, and consulting. Slight decreases in offers were seen both in the manufacturing and in the government and non-profit sectors. Within the area of marketing, there are sometimes pockets where supply exceeds demand. As discussed in the chapters describing specific fields, competition is always strong for advertising and public relations jobs. On the other hand, demand always exists in sales during both good and bad economic times.

The rate of job creation has been low given the rate of economic growth. Some explanations for this are that the productivity gains experienced by many companies reduce the need for more employees, that uncertain economic conditions are causing employers to be cautious about adding new positions, and that hiring and firing costs are growing.

Demand is half of the job market picture; supply is the other half. Supply will not keep pace with demand in most areas, particularly for entry-level workers. As demand grows, the number of workers between the ages of 16 and 24 will decline from 30 percent of the labor force in 1985 to 16 percent in 2000. Participation of women in the work force has leveled off over the past five years. The birth rate has risen, new mothers are slower to return to work, and women are staying in school longer. Employers will have to compete for qualified workers.

Business services is an area of the economy that is growing. Those who work through temporary job agencies are often considered for permanent positions. Nearly 250,000 of Manpower Inc.'s temporary workers were offered permanent positions in 1993. Kelly Services has a program through which those seeking permanent employment are sent to positions for ninety-day tryouts.

GEOGRAPHIC TRENDS IN EMPLOYMENT

The ten states reporting the greatest gains in new non-agricultural jobs in 1993 are (beginning with the highest gain) Utah, Nevada, New Mexico, Idaho, Colorado, Georgia, Florida, North Carolina, South Dakota, and Arizona. Six of the ten are Western states. Cities with the largest job growth are Atlanta and Phoenix. Smaller metropolitan areas with high percentage growth are Provo, Utah and Boise, Idaho. Projections for the future suggest that substantial new job growth will occur in the Midwest.

The fact is that opportunities in marketing careers exist virtually all over the country in companies of all sizes. However, considerable tradeoffs in terms of quality of life, cost of living, and the merits of the job must all be considered. Salaries in marketing tend to be highest where the cost of living is greatest, as expected.

COMPENSATION TRENDS

For new graduates in marketing, salaries increase on average by a couple of hundred to over $3000 a year for the same job, depending on geographical area. Salaries for similar work vary from industry to industry according to industry norms. Since employers within an industry are competing for the same workers, salaries are somewhat consistent, but vary according to the size of the company and the budgets of the different departments. For example, the larger the budget for a certain product, the larger the salaries of those working on the development and promotion of it. Within service industries, firms providing engineering and research services usually pay more than other service firms. The College Placement Council conducts salary surveys of job offers to new college graduates. These surveys can be found in most college career centers.

Figure 11.1 presents average entry-level salaries of graduates with bachelor's degrees in marketing-related areas.

Figure 11.1 Average Salaries for Entry-level Marketing Positions

Field	Salary
Advertising	$20,000
Brand/Product Management	25,000
Buyer/Merchandising	25,000
Customer Service	22,500
Design/Graphic Arts	21,200
Distribution	25,500
Market Research	25,600
Media Planning	22,000
Public Relations	21,700
Purchasing	22,600
Sales	25,300

In researching salary figures it is not unusual for different surveys measuring the same thing to yield different figures because the sample groups differ. The figures reported throughout this book were used because they are consistent with the overall picture presented in a number of sources, but they, too, should be considered approximations.

Salary is only part of the compensation picture. In response to employee demands, employers are offering better and more varied benefit packages. Some of the following items, plus numerous others, may be included in the benefit package: health insurance, dental insurance, life insurance, disability, vacation, sick leave, paid holidays, bonuses, pension plans, employee stock ownership and/or stock purchase plans, and profit-sharing plans. Job applicants must evaluate benefit packages to compute total compensation.

Many important job factors should be considered before an individual accepts a position with a firm. Compensation alone is not enough on which to base employment decisions. In addition to evaluating compensation, company training and development opportunities are also important benefits that should be carefully considered as part of a job offer. It is very important for those entering the job market to investigate companies thoroughly and to ask probing questions during the job interview. Chapter 12 will provide sources of information and job-seeking hints.

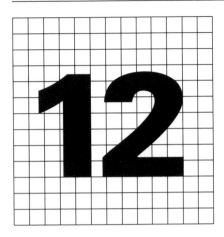

BEGINNING A SUCCESSFUL CAREER IN MARKETING

Job market statistics can be frightening and can shake a graduate's confidence a little. So here's a statistic that might help. Surveys of recent college graduates show that 80 percent of those seeking jobs find work within the first six months and 75 percent of these perceive their jobs to be good career starters. The likelihood of success in a marketing career depends on two things: proper preparation and finding a good job. Preparing oneself for a career in marketing involves getting the best possible education and gaining experience through part-time jobs, internships, and involvement in campus activities. Once prepared to enter the job market, an individual should use a variety of resources to locate the best jobs and acquire some job-finding skills. Many of the best jobs will be in companies graduates have never heard of.

GETTING THE BEST EDUCATION

Depending on an individual's career goal, the required background for a career in marketing may be gained in a high school, vocational school, technical school, community college, college, or university. Educational requirements were discussed throughout the book as part of the specific job descriptions, so this chapter will focus on where to obtain this needed education and training. The majority of the careers discussed in this book require college and university degrees and, in some cases, graduate study.

Probably the most useful source of educational information on programs nationwide is *The College Blue Book*. This five-volume set is particularly useful to those seeking highly specialized programs. The volume entitled *Occupational Education* includes a listing of programs of study in technical schools and community colleges, organized alphabetically by state or by subject area. Another volume, *Degrees Offered by College and Subject*, includes degree programs offered by two-year colleges, four-year colleges, and universities. Other volumes offer narrative descriptions of schools, costs, accreditation, enrollment figures, scholarships, fellowships, grants, loans, and other helpful information.

The College Blue Book is found in the reference section of the library along with many other educational resources. Also available in most college and university libraries is a variety of college catalogs enabling one to compare curricula of different schools offering the degree or program of interest. Education is an important and expensive item. A person should shop for it the way he or she would for any other important, expensive item. Gaining information from counselors, teachers, local colleges and universities, people working in the field, and potential employers is very advisable before selecting an educational program.

One important consideration when choosing a program is whether it has national accreditation. National bodies that accredit these schools are the American Association of Collegiate Schools of Business, the Association of Independent Colleges and Schools, the National Association of Trade and Technical Schools, and the National Home Study Council.

GAINING THE NECESSARY EXPERIENCE

As stressed throughout the book, experience is required for many of the more desirable marketing careers. This experience can be gained through internships and cooperative programs, part-time jobs, and involvement in campus activities.

Internships and Cooperative Programs

Traditional internships are usually three-month summer positions, while co-operative programs (co-ops) last a college quarter, semester, or longer. Internships are sometimes arranged by an interested faculty member and a company manager, and the intern is not always paid. Co-ops, on the other hand, are part of an on-going college program for which students receive both credits and pay. These distinctions aren't as clear any more because companies want to keep interns for longer periods, and they frequently offer paid internships. Many organizations ultimately hire their brightest interns and co-op students. Roughly 26 percent of 1993 graduates were hired from internships or co-op programs. As mentioned earlier, many professional associations offer information on internships available from their member companies. Student membership in a number of professional associations is available at a reduced cost and is worth investigating.

Internships are also advertised on college campuses through placement offices, on billboards, through faculty members, in campus newspapers, and in books. Two such books are listed in Appendix A.

Part-time Jobs

Apart from intern and co-op programs, many students find part-time jobs on their own that offer both pay and experience. Most part-time jobs available to students are in sales. Though these jobs often pay minimum wage and are sometimes hard work, this work experience is very important to prospective employers. For one thing, sales is the most vital aspect of marketing—most activities in marketing are done to maximize sales and profits. Second, employers of part-time students can give important recommendations for full-time jobs. Prospective employers like to hear that a job applicant is reliable, works well with customers and co-workers, and has assumed an assistant manager role on occasion.

Many on-campus jobs can be obtained through student financial aid and job placement services. Throughout every college campus are job boards and student publications advertising openings. Graduate assistantships are available to qualified students. Any opportunity for work experience prior to graduation should be considered because of the strength it lends to the job search for that first, very important, full-time job.

Involvement in Campus Activities

An option to all students is involvement in campus activities and organizations. By joining student business associations and taking a role in student government, students can develop the interpersonal skills needed in most marketing professions. Students who hold leadership positions in campus organizations are particularly sought by corporations. Though grade point average and work experience are very important, they do not always reveal the potential for leadership. Campus leaders rather than scholars are often hired for jobs in many business fields. The very charisma that helps students gain elective offices also scores high marks in job interviews. Participation in organized sports by both men and women also increases the strength of their resumes because learning how to be a good team player is an important lesson. Team playing , along with the acceptance that the coach may not always be right but is never wrong, has probably influenced promotion in corporations as much as academic preparation.

FINDING A GOOD JOB

Competition for good jobs in most areas of marketing is stiff. Graduates should develop job-finding skills as a necessary part of their education. The first full-time job out of college is particularly important because it sometimes sets the direction for an individual's entire career. The first step in the job search is to decide what attributes the individual wants in the job and how the job fits into overall career objectives.

Defining Career Objectives

Since all individuals do not define a good job in the same way, it is important for each job seeker to define what he or she wants in a job before beginning the search. For example, to an entry-level employee, a good job may be one offering growth through a formal company training program or company-financed continuing education; to the physically handicapped person or to a parent with young children, a good job may be one that can be done in the home; to a student, a good job may be part-time or have flexible working hours; to a partner in a dual-career marriage, a good job may be one available locally; to an ambitious woman, a good job may be one in a company employing women managers in key positions. It is very important, therefore for job seekers to have their individual requirements and career goals clearly in mind prior to launching the job search.

Locating Jobs

The task of finding a good job is twofold in that seekers must identify both companies with existing openings and companies for whom they would like to work. The fact that a company does not have an advertised opening does not mean that the company would not create an opening for an outstanding applicant. This makes the job search more complicated, but it also offers the seeker considerably more opportunities. Students should build a network of family, friends, and associates who can refer them to others who might be able to help with their careers.

Many maintain that the way to find excellent jobs is through direct contact with the person who has the authority to hire. One of the best and most widely used books on the subject of job finding is *What Color Is Your Parachute?* by Richard Nelson Bolles. Although this book is not specifically for those seeking marketing careers, the strategies for conducting the job search are universal. This book helps the job seeker organize his or her time and energy and avoid tactics that rarely, if ever, pay off.

Various avenues for locating job opportunities include college placement offices, published job openings, recruiting firms, and computerized search services. These are discussed below.

The college placement office. Prospective college graduates should take advantage of the on-campus interviews arranged by the college placement office. Surveys of companies indicate that roughly 42 percent of their new college hires come from these interviews. They provide an opportunity for a first contact with major company representatives while still on campus. Since these companies are recruiting for current job openings and are willing to hire beginners, young job seekers should definitely take advantage of these opportunities. It is best to sign up early because the company representatives have time for only a limited number of interviews. To prepare for these interviews, individuals should review the information on file in the college placement office. This information, provided by the interviewing companies, often includes annual reports and recruitment materials from which students can glean facts about a particular company and the career opportunities it offers.

Published job openings. A number of sources of listed job openings in business and marketing include *Peterson's Job Opportunities for Business and Liberal Arts Graduates*, *Career Employment Opportunities Directory*, *The Career Guide 1990*, *Career Visions*, and the *CPC Annual*. These books can usually be found in the career planning and placement office of most colleges and universities. They contain a tremendous amount of information, including listings of career opportunities, locations of employment, special training programs available with the companies, benefits, employer profiles, and addresses to write for further information. *Peterson's* also contains information on the job market as well as numerous job-seeking hints.

The *CPC Annual* lists the occupational needs anticipated by approximately one thousand corporations and employers who normally recruit college graduates. One section of the *Annual* lists companies alphabetically and includes phone number, contact person, products and services, date the company was established, the number of employees, a list of available positions, and the location of the available positions. Another section of the *Annual* lists U.S. government agency openings. The *Annual* lists positions for all areas, and it may include openings not listed in other directories. It also provides excellent information on job seeking in general, such as interviewing and resume-writing hints.

Professional journals provide another source of published job openings. Many journals devote a section near the end to advertising job openings. *The Wall Street Journal*, *New York Times*, and other big-city and local newspapers advertise openings, but responding to newspaper advertisements is rarely the way to obtain good jobs.

Recruiting firms. Some job opportunities are listed with recruiting firms. These firms provide needed services to both organizations and applicants. Although it is unusual for a beginner to find a highly desirable job through a recruiting firm and often a sizable chunk of the first month's salary must be paid, these firms do offer some entry-level jobs that enable beginners to get much-needed experience. Some organizations seeking employees assume the charges for the service.

Computerized search services. Computerized search services are gaining in popularity across college campuses. The services vary from school to school, but may include some of the following. Students may call up a list of job openings in their chosen fields. Some systems place student resumes online for companies to review. Other systems allow students to sign up for on-campus interviews by computer. Computer service firms offer these services as well. The *1995 National Job Hotline Directory* offers information organized by state and including some Canada listings that enables job seekers to access more than 3000 employment hotlines 24 hours a day.

Professional association placement services. Many professional associations have placement services including the following:

College Placement Council, Bethlehem, PA, (215) 868-1421

Public Relations Society of America, New York, NY, (212) 995-2230

Society of Research Administrators, Chicago, IL, (312) 661-1700

Women in Communications, Inc., Arlington, VA, (703) 528-4200

Even trade associations without placement services may provide directories of their members free or at a minimal cost. Trade associations can often recommend or supply additional sources of information. Numerous professional associations and their addresses are listed throughout this book.

Job fairs or career days. College recruitment conferences are held in large cities around the country. These career conferences enable new graduates to meet employers who do not normally recruit on their campuses. Many schools and communities sponsor job fairs in which company representatives talk about opportunities within their firms. In addition, many offer seminars in job-seeking skills.

GAINING COMPANY INFORMATION

It is very important for an individual to have knowledge about the specific companies in which he or she will be interviewing.

Published Information

Industry information is extremely valuable to the job seeker. Numerous sources of industry information are available. The current *U.S. Industrial Outlook* analyzes two hundred industries with projections into the future. It is published by the Bureau of Industrial Economics of the U.S. Department of Commerce and can be found in the government documents section of the library. Standard & Poor's Industry Surveys include current and basic analyses for the major domestic industries. The current analysis includes latest industry developments; industry, market, and company statistics; and appraisals of investment outlook. The basic analysis includes prospects for the particular industry, an analysis of trends and problems; spotlights on major segments of the industry; growth in sales and earnings of leading companies in the industry; and other information over a ten-year span. Another excellent source of up-to-date industry information is *The Value Line Investment Survey*.

Many sources focus on specific companies. The *Dun & Bradstreet Directories*, *Moody's Manuals*, and *Thomas's Register* all provide specific company information, such as the address and phone number of the company, what the business produces, its annual sales, and the names of officers and directors. If an individual is interested in the backgrounds of those who make it to the top in a particular company, *Standard & Poor's Register of Corporations, Directors, and Executives* and *Dun & Bradstreet's Reference Book of Corporate Managements* both provide this type of information. These resources are found in public and college libraries in the reference section. Annual and quarterly corporate reports are usually housed in the college career placement offices.

The following is a list of directories that highlight specific areas in marketing:

Standard Directory of Advertising Agencies

Consultants and Consulting Organizations Directory

Dun's Consultant's Directory

Franchise Annual

The Sourcebook of Franchise Opportunities

Bradford's Directory of Marketing Research Agencies and Management Consultants in the United States and the World

The Green Book: International Directory of Marketing Research Houses and Services

O'Dwyer's Directory of Public Relations Firms

Computerized Information

If gathering information quickly is necessary, use the computer. With a few dollars and a little help from the college librarian, a student can research companies using *Disclosure*, a computer database of all U.S. headquartered companies that trade stock publicly. Within seconds, annual and quarterly reports will appear. Other databases include *Dun & Bradstreet's Million Dollar Directory*, *Dun's Market Identifiers*, *Trinet U.S. Business*, *Standard & Poor's Corporate Register*, *Moody's Corporate Profiles*, and *Moody's Corporate News*.

Information on companies can be used by the job seeker to prepare a list of employers to contact, to eliminate companies with low growth potential, to identify a job target for the resume, and to compile a list of intelligent questions that will impress any interviewer.

Other Information

A useful guide to researching prospective employers is the book *Help! My Job Interview Is Tomorrow!* by Mary Ellen Templeton, Neal-Schuman Publishers, Inc., 23 Leonard Street, New York, NY 10013. Another way to gain information about what is happening in companies in the marketing field is by reading professional journals. Along with advertised openings, these journals provide a wealth of information to help the job seeker ask timely and well-informed questions during the interview and to make a final decision on what company would be the best employer. A list of selected journals in marketing areas appears in Appendix B.

THE RESUME

The first contact that most individuals have with a company is the resume. It has to be good or a job applicant may never gain an interview. Every statement should show how an applicant is qualified for the position he or she seeks. As a reflection of one's skill in written communication, it is a perfect way to bias the interviewer on an applicant's behalf before he or she walks through the door. A resume is basically a sales device. It should do three things. First, it should emphasize the most positive features in an individual's background, such as maintaining an A average in college. Second, it should stress work experience and positive contributions to former employers. Third, it should describe positive personal attributes and abilities. The best resumes are written by individuals themselves rather than by professional resume-preparation services. Only individuals can present themselves in their best light and sound truthful doing it. It is wise, however, to get some editorial help from a career counselor or other skilled writer since the resume should make the best possible impression.

Resume Basics

The following are some basic hints for writing a good resume:

1. People usually skim resumes. Too many numbers, too much verbiage, poor spacing, and unclear headings all make a resume difficult to skim. Strongest positive points should be made first.

2. No matter how terrific a person is or how much experience he or she has had, a resume for a new college graduate should not exceed one page. A person should only use two pages if their experience is sufficient to qualify them for a management position and/or after excluding all non-essential information, such as information on hobbies. One should stick to the facts and save philosophy for the interview, if asked about it. Unnecessary words such as "I," "he," or "she" should be eliminated. Resumes are usually written in phrases—not complete sentences.

3. Action words such as "coordinated," "supervised," and "developed" should be used. A resume should be oriented toward results and accomplishments rather than duties. The tone should be as positive as the content.

4. The resume should be free of spelling or grammatical errors and neatly typed or professionally printed on white or ivory rag paper. No fancy binders should be used.

5. Salaries, reasons for termination, references, supervisors' names, politics, religion, race, ethnic background, sex, height, weight, and pictures should be excluded.

6. An individually typed cover letter should be used each time a resume is sent to a prospective employer. The letter should be addressed to a specific person rather than "Personnel Director" whenever possible. In it, the applicant introduces himself or herself, explains the reason

for writing, describes potential contributions to the company, and requests an interview. A job target should be identified in the cover letter if a target resume is not used. Copies of all letters sent should be kept in one file folder; responses requiring action by the applicant should be kept in a second; and rejection letters should be kept in a third.

With the above basics clearly in mind, the applicant should write a resume that is a summary of his or her education, work experience, interests, career goals, and any other information that qualifies that individual for the position sought.

Resume Formats

Different formats may be used in developing a resume. The type of format used depends on the background of the individual.

Chronological resumes. A commonly used format is a chronological arrangement of educational and work experiences, each listed separately with the most recent experience first. If an applicant is seeking a job that is a natural progression from former jobs and has a good work history with growth and development, this is a good format to use. However, if an applicant's former work history consists of part-time jobs while in college, there is a better format—the functional arrangement.

Functional resumes. A resume organized around functional or topical headings stresses competencies. Such headings as "Research" and "Marketing" enable an individual to include coursework, special projects, and work experience in these areas. These headings are geared to the type of position the applicant is seeking. Actual work experience is included at the bottom of the resume. Both functional and chronological resumes can be used for broad career objectives.

Targeted resumes. A type of resume used widely today is the targeted resume. Jobs have become more specific and highly defined than they used to be. Beginners who are aware of the job market will have developed some special areas of expertise in order to make them viable applicants for some of the best positions. The job target is clearly stated along with specific areas of expertise related to the applicant's ability to do the job.

Which resume format is best is a function of the applicant's experience and career objectives. A good resume increases the likelihood that an individual will be contacted for an interview. This contact is often by phone, so the job seeker should keep a pad and pen beside the phone to record any information from such calls. The more organized and in control an applicant appears, the more impressed prospective employers will be.

An excellent book for information on resume writing is *Resumes for College Students and Recent Graduates*, published by VGM Career Horizons, NTC Publishing Group, 4255 W. Touhy Avenue, Lincolnwood, IL 60646-1975.

PREPARING FOR THE INTERVIEW

Preparing for a job interview involves a lot more than putting on clothes. An earlier section described sources of information on specific companies. It is sometimes possible for an individual to obtain a schedule of his or her visit to the company in advance, including the names and titles of the interviewers. If any are senior managers, their backgrounds could be researched in an industry *Who's Who* or another source, and some aspect of this background could be casually referred to during the interview. A job candidate could also request a sample copy of any standard employee newsletter, relevant company publication, or an annual company stockholder report.

Since the applicant has some time during the interview process to ask questions, it is best to have developed a list of critical questions, some based on the pre-interview research. Examples of such questions include the following. What type of performance appraisal system is used? How is the company's career development system set up, and what are some common career paths within the company? How are new workers trained and developed? How long has the prospective supervisor held that position? What is the management style of the company? In what direction is future growth anticipated? In short, any information that the applicant has been unable to gain in advance that might heavily affect his or her career development should be learned in the interview, if possible.

Conservative dress—without looking uniformed—is usually safe attire for a job interview. Women might wear a simply tailored suit, a neat hairdo, plain jewelry, and moderate makeup and perfume. Men might wear a conservative suit, shirt, and tie. Polished shoes, trimmed and styled hair, and clean fingernails are all important.

Posture is significant, as are all types of body language. A firm handshake, good eye contact, poise, ease, and manners all contribute to a positive interview. The novice job applicant might even improve his or her overall performance at a job interview by practicing beforehand in front of a mirror.

A portfolio of college experiences might be useful to show to a prospective employer at the job interview. This portfolio can include best class papers; descriptions of projects completed for class, internships, or jobs; and fliers from events in which a student participated or helped organize such as seminars or club fund-raising events. Anything related to the job should be in the portfolio.

THE INTERVIEW

Each corporation has a culture of its own. An applicant's ability to fit into this culture is often the key to being hired. Sizing up the corporate culture is something an applicant can do by walking into a lobby. Is there elaborate security or a club-like atmosphere? Is the coffee served in fine china or plastic cups? Do the executives sometimes answer their own phones? Are only degrees and certificates displayed in the offices, or family photos as well? The applicant's ability to discern the degree of formality or informality and modify interview behaviors accordingly might make the difference between a job offer or disappointment. The fact is that managers are not only looking for levels of experience but for types of individuals who would fit comfortably into the organization. In other words, chemistry between candidate and interviewer is critical. Both need to determine whether or not they would like to work together daily. This is a highly subjective factor.

The applicants most likely to be hired are effective communicators both on professional and personal levels. Marketing graduates have an edge because most of them know how to sell things—including themselves. They are warm, outgoing, enthusiastic, and self-confident. Both the applicant and interviewer are under stress. The more relaxed both manage to be during the interview, the better the interview will be and the more information will be exchanged. The interviewer is looking at both substance, which is basically a person's past performance, and style, which includes communication skills, poise, self-confidence, and motivation. Broad questions such as "How would you describe yourself ?" and "How can you contribute to our organization?" reveal the applicant's values and personality and how the applicant organizes his or her thoughts. How a person fields questions also shows performance under pressure, quickness, energy, and sense of humor.

In general, employers regard specific skills and experience as more important qualifications than educational background. Such skills as written and verbal communications, related work experience, and knowledge of the functions of the company are very important. This is not to say that grade point average and coursework are not scrutinized also. The point is that most employers care more about what you can do for their company than what you have learned in college, so in both the resume and the interview, job seekers should focus on the skills they possess and the value of these skills to the company.

Often a preliminary interview is conducted by a member of the human resources department who is skilled in interview techniques. This interview determines whether or not a candidate will fit into the corporate culture. If this interview goes well for the candidate, a second interview is conducted by the manager of the department in which the applicant would work. An applicant should ask questions as the interview progresses or, if the interviewer shows a high need for structure, should wait until asked if there are any questions. The applicant's questions should emphasize professional growth and work-related activities. Such topics as salary and benefits should be discussed after the job is offered. Some bargaining may then occur, particularly if the applicant has another offer in hand.

Ironically, most applicants forget to ask for the job. An applicant should both ask for the job and thank the interviewer. Some indication of when the applicant will hear from the company should be given. The interest that an interviewer shows in an applicant does not mean that a job will be offered. It is standard operating procedure; the interviewer is building goodwill and keeping the applicant interested. Applicants should go on as many interviews as possible and carefully compare companies and offers, no matter how well a first interview goes or how certain an applicant is that a job will be offered. Additional offers not only provide an individual with choices but give some leverage to the applicant who can then bargain for salary and benefits.

A person is his or her own best resource. By using good judgment in choosing and planning a career, by gaining information from a variety of sources, by relying on well-formulated questions as well as intuition in accepting a job, an individual can increase the chances for success in a marketing career.

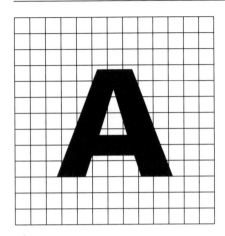

RESEARCHING CAREERS IN MARKETING

Many libraries have computerized databases that list books, articles, software, government documents, and every imaginable source of information for researching specific interest areas. With the help of technology and your librarian, you can browse electronically. The following list contains some current sources you might want to seek out in your library or career center.

Basye, Anne. *Opportunities in Direct Marketing Careers*. Lincolnwood, Ill.: VGM Career Horizons, 1993.

Basye, Anne. *Opportunities in Telemarketing Careers*. Lincolnwood, Ill.: VGM Career Horizons, 1994.

Field, Shelly. *Career Opportunities in Advertising and Public Relations*. New York, N.Y.: Facts on File, Inc., 1993.

Ganim, Barbara A. *How to Approach an Advertising Agency & Walk Away with the Job You Want*. Lincolnwood, Ill.: NTC Publishing Group, 1993.

Internships—*Advertising, Marketing, Public Relations, & Sales*. Hawthorne, N.J.: Career Press, Inc., 1989.

Internships, the Guide to On-the-Job Training Opportunities for Students and Adults. Princeton, N.J.: Peterson's Guides, 1992.

Job Opportunities in Business 1994. Princeton, N.J.: Peterson's Guides, 1992.

Making It in Advertising: An Insider's Guide to Career Opportunities. New York, N.Y.: Macmillan Publishing Company, 1993.

Making It in Public Relations: An Insider's Guide to Career Opportunities. New York, N.Y.: Macmillan Publishing Company, 1993.

Marketing and Sales Career Directory. Detroit, Mich.: Gale Research, Inc., 1991.

Occupational Outlook Handbook. 1994-1995 ed. Lincolnwood, Ill.: NTC Publishing Group, 1994.

Pattis, S. William. *Careers in Advertising*. Lincolnwood, Ill.: VGM Career Horizons, 1990.

Petras, Kathryn and Ross. *Jobs '94*. New York, N.Y.: Simon & Schuster, Inc., 1993.

Peterson's Job Opportunities for Business and Liberal Arts Graduates 1991. 8th edition. Princeton, N.J.: Peterson's Guides, 1991.

Public Relations Career Directory. Detroit, Mich.: Gale Research, Inc., 1991.

Resumes for Sales & Marketing Careers. Lincolnwood, Ill.: VGM Career Horizons, 1991.

Steinberg, Margery. *Opportunities in Marketing Careers*. Lincolnwood, Ill.: VGM Career Horizons, 1993.

VGM's Career Encyclopedia. Lincolnwood, Ill.: VGM Career Horizons, 1992.

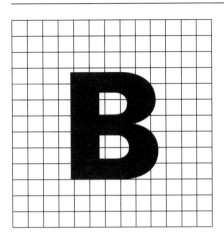

JOURNALS IN MARKETING AND RELATED AREAS

One of the best ways to keep up with current trends in marketing fields is by reading professional journals. Most of these journals are available in larger community and college libraries. *Ulrich's International Periodicals Directory* and *The Standard Periodical Directory* offer extensive lists of journals in print in the areas of marketing, advertising, and public relations. A partial list of journals appears below.

Advertising Age
American Demographics
American Salesman
Bank Marketing
Brandweek
Business Marketing
Catalog Age
Chain Store Age Executive
Communication World
Communications News
Direct Marketing
Discount Merchandiser
Entrepreneurship Theory and Practice
European Journal of Marketing
Folio
Industrial Distribution
Industrial Marketing Management
International Journal of Research in Marketing

International Journal of Retail and Distribution Management
International Marketing Review
Journal of Advertising
Journal of Advertising Research
Journal of Business & Industrial Marketing
Journal of Consumer Marketing
Journal of Consumer Research
Journal of Direct Marketing
Journal of Marketing
Journal of Marketing Research
Journal of Product Innovation Management
Journal of Product and Brand Management
Journal of Professional Services Marketing
Journal of the Academy of Marketing Science
Journal of the Market Research Society
Marketing
Marketing Consultants
Marketing Direct Journal
Mediaweek
Public Relations Journal
Public Relations Quarterly
Public Relations Review
Sales & Marketing Management
Sales & Marketing Management in Canada
Target Marketing
Telemarketing

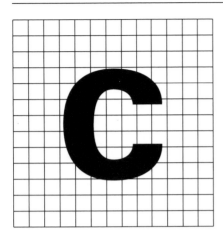

SOURCES OF INFORMATION FOR JOB SEEKERS

Many resources were incorporated into sections of this text. In addition to those already listed, numerous other sources of information relevant to job seekers are available in government documents and reference sections of public and university libraries. The *Directory of Directories* is useful in identifying directories containing information in specific fields. These sources can be best explored with the help of the reference librarian. A sampling of the more common sources of general information are listed below.

GOVERNMENT

Guide to Federal Jobs
National Directory of State Agencies
Working For Your Uncle

BUSINESS AND INDUSTRY

Almanac of American Employers
Canadian Almanac and Directory
Career Employment Opportunities
Corporate Jobs Outlook
Job Hunter's Sourcebook
Job Seekers Guide to Private and Public Companies
O'Dwyer's Directory of Public Relations Firms
100 Best Companies to Sell For
100 Best Companies to Work For

Marketing & Sales Career Directory
National Job-Finding Guide
Peterson's Job Opportunities for Business and Liberal Arts Graduates
Sheldon's Retail Directory of the United States and Canada
Summer Employment Directory of the United States
Thomas Register of American Manufacturers
The Career Guide—Dun's Employment Opportunities Directory
Trade Directories of the World
World Wide Chamber of Commerce Directory

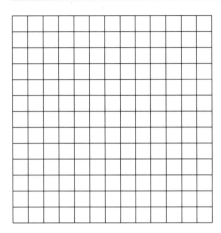

BIBLIOGRAPHY

"Are Good Causes Good Marketing." *Business Week*, March 21, 1994, 64–66.

"Benchmarking Salaries." *Sales & Marketing Management*, April 1994, v. 146, 38.

"B-Schools Bitten By the Global Bug." *Business Week*, October 25, 1993, 106–107.

"Congratulations, Exporter! Now About Getting Paid..." *Business Week*, January 17, 1994, 98.

"Corporate America's New Lesson Plan." *Business Week*, October 25, 1993, 102–104.

CPC Salary Survey. July 1994. Bethlehem PA: College Placement Council, Inc., 1994.

"Database Marketing." *Business Week*, September 5, 1994, 56–62.

"Dream Jobs All Over." *Business Week*, April 4, 1994, 34–36.

Dumaine, Brian. "A Knockout Year for CEO Pay." *Fortune*, July 25, 1994, 94–103.

"Eighth Annual Salary Survey." *Public Relations Journal*, July 1993, v. 49, 10–17.

Farnham, Alan. "America's Most Admired Company." *Fortune*, February 7, 1994, 50–54.

Fierman, Jaclyn. "The Death and Rebirth of the Salesman." *Fortune*, July 25, 1994, 80–91.

Gutner, Toddi. "Junior Entrepreneurs." *Forbes*, May 9, 1994, 188–189.

"Inside the Black Network." *Business Week*, November 29, 1993, 70–81.

"Invasion of the Retail Snatchers." *Business Week*, May 9, 1994, 72–74.

Jacob, Rahul. "Why Some Customers Are More Equal Than Others." *Fortune*, September 19, 1994, 215–224.

Keenan, William, Jr. "Compensation—In Search of Equity." *Sales & Marketing Management*, November 1993, 82–86.

Lenzner, Robert. "Starting 'Em Young." *Forbes*, September 12, 1994, 70–72.

"Lock the Doors, It's EDS." *Business Week*, September 19, 1994, 36.

"Making the Middleman an Endangered Species." *Business Week*, June 6, 1994, 114–115.

Mullich, Joe. "'90s the Time for a Career in Marketing." *Business Marketing*, February 1994, 15–18.

Novack, Janet. "Is Lean, Mean?" *Forbes*, August 15, 1994, 88–89.

Occupational Outlook Handbook. 1992–1993 ed. Lincolnwood, IL: NTC Publishing Group, 1992.

"Opportunity Knocks." *Worth,* April 1994, 34.

O'Reilly, Brian. "The New Face of Small Business." *Fortune*, May 2, 1994, 82–88.

Peterson's Job Opportunities for Business and Liberal Arts Graduates 1991. Princeton, NJ: Peterson's Guides, 1991.

"Salary Survey." *Advertising Age*, December 6, 1993, S-1–S-10.

Saporito, Bill. "Where the Global Action Is." *Fortune*, Autumn/Winter 1993, 63–77.

Sellers, Patricia. "Do You Need Your Ad Agency?" *Fortune*, November 15, 1993, 147–156.

Sellers, Patricia. "The Best Way to Reach Your Buyers." *Fortune*, Autumn/Winter 1993, 13–17.

Sookdeo, Ricardo. "Oh, Baby! What a Year for Products." *Fortune*, December 27, 1993, 90–95.

"Small Is Powerful." *Business Week/Enterprise*, 1993, 66–98.

Smith, Lee. "Landing That First Real Job." *Fortune*, May 16, 1994, 58–60.

"Stuck! How Companies Cope When They Can't Raise Prices." *Business Week*, November 15, 1993, 146–155.

"Teens—Here Comes the Biggest Wave Yet." *Business Week*, April 11, 1994, 76–86.

"That Eye–Popping Executive Pay." *Business Week*, April 25, 1994, 52–58.

"The Craze for Consultants." *Business Week*, July 25, 1994, 60–66.

"The Economics of Aging." *Business Week*, September 12, 1994, 60–68.

"The Entertainment Economy." *Business Week*, March 14, 1994, 58–66.

"The Entrepreneurs." *Business Week/Enterprise*, 1993, 102–143.

"The Insider." *Fortune*, May 2, 1994, 14.

Tully, Shawn. "Teens the Most Global Market of All." *Fortune*, May 16, 1994, 90–97.

"What Is an Ad in the Interactive Future?" *Business Week*, May 2, 1994, 103.

"Women Entrepreneurs." *Business Week*, April 18, 1994, 104–105.

"Workers May Get Scarce, But Nobody's Scared." *Business Weekly*, July 11, 1994, 95–98.

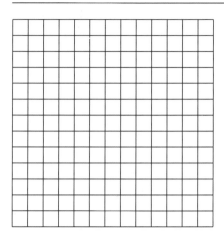

JOB INDEX

VGM CAREER BOOKS

CAREER DIRECTORIES
Careers Encyclopedia
Dictionary of Occupational
   Titles
Occupational Outlook
   Handbook

CAREERS FOR
Animal Lovers
Bookworms
Computer Buffs
Crafty People
Culture Lovers
Environmental Types
Film Buffs
Foreign Language Aficionados
Good Samaritans
Gourmets
History Buffs
Kids at Heart
Nature Lovers
Night Owls
Number Crunchers
Plant Lovers
Shutterbugs
Sports Nuts
Travel Buffs

CAREERS IN
Accounting; Advertising;
Business; Child Care;
Communications; Computers;
Education; Engineering;
the Environment; Finance;
Government; Health Care;
High Tech; Journalism; Law;
Marketing; Medicine;
Science; Social &
Rehabilitation Services

CAREER PLANNING
Admissions Guide to Selective
   Business Schools
Beating Job Burnout
Beginning Entrepreneur
Career Planning &
   Development for College
   Students & Recent Graduates
Career Change

Careers Checklists
Cover Letters They Don't
   Forget
Executive Job Search Strategies
Guide to Basic Cover Letter
   Writing
Guide to Basic Resume Writing
Guide to Temporary
   Employment
Job Interviews Made Easy
Joyce Lain Kennedy's Career
   Book
Out of Uniform
Resumes Made Easy
Slam Dunk Resumes
Successful Interviewing for
   College Seniors
Time for a Change

CAREER PORTRAITS
Animals	Nursing
Cars	Sports
Computers	Teaching
Music	Travel

GREAT JOBS FOR
Communications Majors
English Majors
Foreign Language Majors
History Majors
Psychology Majors

HOW TO
Approach an Advertising
   Agency and Walk Away with
   the Job You Want
Bounce Back Quickly After
   Losing Your Job
Choose the Right Career
Find Your New Career Upon
   Retirement
Get & Keep Your First Job
Get Hired Today
Get into the Right Business
   School
Get into the Right Law School
Get People to Do Things Your
   Way
Have a Winning Job Interview

Hit the Ground Running in
   Your New Job
Improve Your Study Skills
Jump Start a Stalled Career
Land a Better Job
Launch Your Career in TV
   News
Make the Right Career Moves
Market Your College Degree
Move from College into a
   Secure Job
Negotiate the Raise You
   Deserve
Prepare a Curriculum Vitae
Prepare for College
Run Your Own Home Business
Succeed in College
Succeed in High School
Write a Winning Resume
Write Successful Cover Letters
Write Term Papers & Reports
Write Your College Application
   Essay

OPPORTUNITIES IN
This extensive series provides
detailed information on nearly
150 individual career fields.

RESUMES FOR
Advertising Careers
Banking and Financial Careers
Business Management Careers
College Students &
   Recent Graduates
Communications Careers
Education Careers
Engineering Careers
Environmental Careers
50 + Job Hunters
Health and Medical Careers
High School Graduates
High Tech Careers
Law Careers
Midcareer Job Changes
Sales and Marketing Careers
Scientific and Technical Careers
Social Service Careers
The First-Time Job Hunter

VGM Career Horizons
a division of *NTC Publishing Group*
4255 West Touhy Avenue
Lincolnwood, Illinois 60646–1975